despair

A MOMENT OR
A WAY OF LIFE?

C. STEPHEN EVANS

Bernard Ramm

INTER-VARSITY PRESS
DOWNERS GROVE, ILLINOIS 60515

InterVarsity Press is the
book publishing division of
Inter-Varsity Christian
Fellowship.

ISBN 0-87784-699-5
Library of Congress Catalog
Card Number: 78-169906

Printed in the United
States of America

To Charles and Pearline Evans

who first pushed me along the way

contents

in
the face
of
death:
despair

chapter 1

What is existentialism? Often at parties or social gatherings, when it becomes known I am a student of philosophy, I am asked this question. Usually I try to evade the query. I say it is too difficult, too complicated to explain, or something of that sort. But though this may be true in a way, it is false in a far deeper sense. To tell what existentialism is all about, I have only to share an experience I have had, an experience not unique to me, but one which I believe everyone has had at some time to some degree. I cannot hope to truly describe this experience. I can only hope to engender the memory of that experience in you, for if you have not felt what I felt, you shall not understand.

An Evening in Front of the Tube

It was late at night, around 1:30 A.M. I was watching a late night movie on television, a harmless enough diversion. Television is such a marvelous thing, surely the most wonderful means man has ever found to amuse himself. The movie was a diversion from myself, a means of stepping back from the cares and worries of the day. Like a true child of the twentieth century I was attempting to put my life at a distance, to place it on the little screen in front of me and enjoy it while it ran past.

But as that movie ended, my life returned to me and once more became for me a problem, or rather a mystery. What is the meaning of human existence? The mystery does not merely concern some vague entity called "human existence." The real mystery is *my* existence; that *I* exist at all.

The movie had been a western, filled with deaths and killings and loves which were not real to me. After all, it was only a movie. But somehow one villainous character stuck with me. Charley was a killer who derived a sadistic thrill from killing. His pleasure came from the feeling that each time he killed, he had committed an act which was irreversible. This was a feeling which gave him an almost sexual gratification, evidencing the power he possessed within him. Regardless of the horror and disgust which Charley produced in me, I was struck by the phenomenon he pointed to—the irreversible.

Of course death is irreversible. The act which brings about death accomplishes something which cannot be changed. But the least amount of insight reveals that this phenomenon is not limited to killing. It is a paradigm for every human act, for every act is irreversible; it possesses a finality which our wishes and desires cannot change.

Time is irreversible. A situation confronts us, we act and then the thing is settled. I, Stephen Evans, am confronted with the fact that I have a free evening, which I can devote to loving and sharing with my wife, to reading and reflection on the subject of immortality or to watching situation comedies on television. I must choose, or else by not choosing I will choose to do nothing. In any case, after this evening, it will remain true for eternity that Stephen Evans did so-and-so on the evening of February 16, 1970. Time will compel me to go on, leaving me with the responsibility for my action and its consequences.

Time constrains me and compels me on all sides. I was born in 1948. I cannot return to the innocence of boyhood or jump to the placidity of middle-age. I am right here, now, hedged everywhere by this here and this now.

Time the jailer drags me relentlessly along, kicking and struggling. His road leads always in one direction—age and death. Just as I now look back on my boyhood, so someday I shall look back on my young manhood, perhaps with regret, perhaps with nostalgia. But someday, the jailer willing, I shall be old and just as imprisoned by time as I am now. I shall be old without choosing to be old and without possibility of returning to my youth.

I can even picture my old age. Perhaps I will sit in a chair all day long, unable to feed and clothe myself. Then I shall *know* that my life is nearly over. For now, I can disguise the fact that death faces me all the time. I can tell myself that I am young, that death is a long way off because I have a long life ahead of me. But is the difference really so great between a few weeks and a few years? Regardless of whether the time be two weeks or fifty years, it is certain that a time is coming when I will be forced to recognize that my life is completed, finished, done. Time will tell me bluntly that I have lived my life, that I have received my due from the earth.

And then what? That night, after the light on the tube dwindled away, I lay back in my bed and stared at the darkened ceiling. I felt time dragging me inexorably towards death; I felt the panic of a man in a car out of control, hurtling toward a precipice on a dark night, the steering locked, the brakes useless. Ahead loomed a plunge into an unknown abyss. In view of my death, what is the meaning of my life? What meaning can time have?

My mind shouted the answers. There is a God. Death is not the end. There must be more. But for a moment my soul did not hear the answers. I gazed directly into the hideous jaws of nothingness, and I was filled with a dread inspired by nothing human. There it was, the abyss yawning in front of me. Time was dragging me closer every hour, every minute, every infinitesimal fraction of a second. I shuddered, I sweated, I wanted to scream and flail against the flux sweeping me along, ever nearer.

In the words of a popular song, "Is *that* all there is?" Are all man's religions and philosophies merely his attempts to deceive himself, convince himself that life is not the bad joke it really is? Do they stem from a cowardice which refuses to face the bluntness of reality? Are they only another form of that "ordinary" way of life which makes "death" an abstract thing which happens to "everyone," but not something to be faced directly by each individual man?

Twentieth-Century Man

This experience which I have so feebly tried to recall for you expresses as best I can the attitude of passionate concern for human existence which I believe is characteristic of existentialism. Implicit here are many of the themes which recur in existentialist literature and philosophy: despair, dread, death and the absurd. Existentialism involves a recognition of and concern for the plight of man in the twentieth century.

What is the plight of twentieth-century man? On reflection it would appear that the human condition is the same in every age. Perhaps the uniqueness of twentieth-century man lies in the bomb, in pollution, in the prospect of man's putting an end to all human existence. Though these problems certainly are essential aspects of the anxiety of twentieth-century man, they cannot be the complete story. Though their portents are doom and destruction on a vast scale, the uniqueness is only numerical. From the perspective of the individual, death, destruction and misery have always been plentiful. Twentieth-century man has the same destiny as his predecessors. Each man will die. He will die only once, and he will die by himself, whether surrounded by his family in a hospital bed or accompanied by the entire human race in a fiery, nuclear holocaust.

The uniqueness of the twentieth century lies not in the universe which faces man, but in the man who faces the universe. For the first time man faces his problems *alone*, all alone in the universe. *God* is dead. He died in Europe in the nineteenth century, though the news was a little slow crossing the Atlantic. This has been widely proclaimed, and it cannot be denied that it is true in one profound and important sense. *For twentieth-century man,* God is dead. The concept of God has become meaningless to him. The person of God has become irrelevant to his beliefs and way of life. The

onrushing wheels of positivistic science coupled
with a naive and optimistic naturalism have effectively dismembered the carcass of a comprehensive
world and life view which had upheld man for
centuries.

It is widely recognized that Western man today
lives in the post-Christian era. What has not been so
widely recognized is that man perished along with
God.

An anthology of twentieth-century philosophy
is entitled *The Age of Analysis*, as if to imply that
the distinguishing characteristic of twentieth-century man has been the keen, probing mind of the
scientist, breaking down reality into its ultimate
constituent parts. Without minimizing the overwhelming importance of science, from the point of
view of someone truly concerned with human
existence, a far truer title would be *The Age of
Despair*, symbolizing the crumbling of man's world
into meaningless fragments. Despair is at the crux
of existentialist thought. This despair is no idle
pessimism, but the result of an honest appraisal of
man's condition in modern society. The question
which we must put to existentialist writers is the
status of hope in this modern world. Is despair the
final word, or can this honest facing of man's
plight be the prelude to an authentic hope?

To understand the despair of twentieth-century
man one must understand the slogan of Friedrich
Nietzsche in the nineteenth century, which was

given the status of a movement in the 1960s. "God is dead." *Not*, "there is no God." God was once alive, but he has died. His spectre haunts the mind of twentieth-century man. God is gone but not forgotten. Today's folk songs, protest chants, poetry, novels, drama and even obscenities are filled with references to the God who man refuses to believe exists. In the novels of Jean Paul Sartre, God plays a central role, not by his presence, but by his absence. God ought to exist, but he does not and his absence pervades Sartre's world.

How truly God is absent from the twentieth century can be seen in its eschatological literature, its visions of the world towards which man is inevitably moving. Previously, from the time of St. Thomas More's *Utopia*, many idealistic social reformers had carried with them a shining vision of a better world for man, a world with justice for all, with poverty and ignorance banished. These visions were ultimately grounded in the Christian view of time; the belief that Providence was in control of history and that therefore good would ultimately triumph over evil. Nineteenth-century English re-formers like Wilberforce and Shaftesbury were particularly endued with the fervent belief that they were helping to "bring in on earth the kingdom of God."

These utopian visions are a stark contrast to the *dis*topias of the twentieth century, the age of *1984* and *Brave New World*. In the United States, leftists, radicals, right-wingers and believers of all stripes and colors embrace their causes with a stark, cynical pessimism. This pessimism many times culminates in a sense of futility, leading to drugs, mysticism, apathy or "blind rage" *a la* the Weatherman faction of the SDS. It is a far cry from William Wilberforce to *Revolution for the Hell of It.* The twentieth century, having lost God, believes it has lost the future.

The Nineteenth Century: The Transition to Despair

The transitional movement of modern thought to despair is perhaps best illumined through a comparison of Fyodor Dostoevsky, Nietzsche and Sartre. In *The Brothers Karamazov* Dostoevsky expresses his tormented doubts as to whether God exists. This is for him no mere intellectual game; the stakes are the very meaning of morality, art and life itself. In the mind of Dmitry Karamazov, who is contemplating the horrible crime of murdering his father, Dostoevsky plants an audacious thought: "If there is no God, then everything is permitted." Dostoevsky himself could not accept this conclusion, and he retained his faith in the God of the Russian Orthodox Church.

With Friedrich Nietzsche we find a far different temperament. He seizes on what was for Dostoevsky a tragedy and embraces it joyfully and whole-heartedly. The meaning of *Thus Spoke Zarathustra* is plain. God is dead, but this is no tragedy. The way is open for man to become God, for the Superman to appear to create new values. "Let your will say, 'the Superman *shall be* the meaning of the earth.' " The old values and the old God are exposed as merely weak creations of man. Man did not find God; he created him in his own image and now God has been put to death. Now the Superman is free to create values which will be true values. Man can find meaning *here*, in the earth, not in some extra-terrestrial pie-in-the-sky. Man is free from the God who stands over him and says, "Thou shalt not." Free, gloriously free, from the strictures of an imposed morality.

But alas for man. The freedom bequeathed him by Nietzsche was a curse, not a blessing. In the twisted distortions and grotesque misuse of Nietzsche's philosophy by the Nazis, we see how some used this radical freedom.

Two French Existentialists: Sartre and Marcel

In the philosophical and literary works of Jean Paul Sartre, the nature of this freedom in a world without God is mercilessly exposed. Man is free, *doomed* to be free, sentenced to total freedom. Man is alone, but worse than alone, he is totally unnecessary. His existence is superfluous, gratuitous in a world in which there is no *reason* for anything. There is no *reason* why a man should choose to marry, rather than remain celibate, no *reason* why a man should love, rather than hate, no *reason* why a man should choose to feed and care for a child, rather than snuff out that child's existence, no *reason* why a man should choose to go on living instead of killing himself. Ultimately, there is no reason for any action, for any decision. The agony of man's freedom lies here. For though man is totally free to choose, there is no reason why he should choose one thing over another. And yet, since he is the sole author of his choice, he is totally responsible for that choice!

In every decision, says Sartre, every man stands alone, with complete freedom. When he chooses, he is choosing for the whole of mankind. He is deciding what right and wrong shall be. He is saying, "Any man, when confronted by this situation, ought to do as I have done." This is the meaning of any decision. But there is *nothing* to help man choose. The responsibility is awesome, but the decision is totally arbitrary. There are no values which man finds embedded in the nature of things, no knowledge of good and evil, to tell man that this thing is right and that thing is wrong. He himself decides what is right and what is wrong, and it is this knowledge which fills the chooser with anguish, the terrible anguish of a man who must make a decision for the whole world, yet who has no basis for his decision. What prevents a man from deciding that gassing Jews is right? What, indeed?

There can be little doubt that Sartre has given a

powerful description of a world without God. And, to be sure, this is the world he sees around him, the world in which he lives. But from this, it does not necessarily follow that Sartre is correct, that there is no God and that the human situation is really as he describes it.

Logically, there are two alternatives. Perhaps there is no God and Sartre has given a profound description of human existence. But it is also possible that God truly exists, but not for Sartre. That is, God may be really "there" but Sartre may never have encountered him because he has chosen to cut himself off from God. Sartre could be imprisoned in a godless world of his own making.

This is the view of another French existentialist, Gabriel Marcel. The keynote of Marcel's vision of life is hope. For Marcel the experience of despair can become the prelude and vehicle for an authentic hope which far transcends mere naive optimism.

Marcel is sensitive to that characteristic of modern society which many thinkers have termed "alienation." Man has become a conglomeration of functions, small cogs for the giant wheels of modern society. He serves an industrial function, perhaps at a meaningless job. He serves a biological function, too often on a merely biological level; the collapse of marriage and the home, for example, has degraded the sexual act to a purely physical encounter. He serves his social functions as consumer, voter, taxpayer, etc. In all of his activities, bereft of meaning and significance, he has become a function. He has ceased to live as a *person*.

Caught in the grip of these social forces, man desperately needs to be awakened to what it means to be truly human. An experience of despair which tears a man out of himself and forces him to question the meaning of his existence can be the trigger for a new and authentic way of life. It can engender in a man an acute realization of what he has lost, and thus open his eyes to what is of real value and significance in life. Marcel passionately affirms that in love, faith and hope, man encounters something that transcends the pseudo-scientific category of the "purely natural." In certain crucially significant human experiences man may encounter transcendence, the presence of the Beyond which renders human existence significant here and now. For Marcel the road can lead from despair to hope—and to God.

Is Hope Really Possible?

Hope is a problematic concept for twentieth-century man. Even in the United States, that boundless reservoir of optimism and progress, it is widely recognized that there is a deep-seated crisis of nerve. Haynes Johnson, in a news story for the *Washington Post* news service on May 17, 1970, analyzed what he termed a national "crisis of confidence" which he said affected every age group and economic class in America.

Some call this "a loss of faith in America," as if the United States possessed some guarantee, exempting her from the historical situation which faces all nations and all people. Some blame the situation on left-wingers, some on right-wingers, some on blacks, some on prejudiced whites, some on college students, some on "Middle America." Perhaps the true source of discontent is simply a recognition that life is not what it ought to be, that many things which promised satisfaction cannot make good on those promises. There ought to be *more* to life. The result is an uneasiness, a fear or perhaps an anxiety in the hearts of Americans which is perhaps a prelude to the despair which has already gripped many sensitive thinkers and artists, in both Europe and America.

Can I hope? For what can I hope? In what—or whom—can I hope? In the midst of despair these questions are flung up. These are intensely personal questions, to which no man can adduce universal, compelling logical arguments to justify his choice. At most, we can but shine a light for a brother; with him alone lies the responsibility of choosing the way. I have chosen a way, which, with the humility and openness which befits a traveler on this earth, I believe with all my heart to be the true way. This pathway to hope indeed lies through the valley of despair, and it is there our journey must begin.

the
despair
of
morality

chapter 2

Perhaps the dominant characteristic of a despairing world is that it is a world where there are no absolutes, no stationary lighthouses by which man may steer in his perilous voyage. This is particularly true of moral values. Perhaps in this area the agony of being alone in the universe is best portrayed in literature.

Dostoevsky's Dilemma: Is Everything Permitted?

Dostoevsky's *The Brothers Karamazov* is a preface to the agony of post-Christian man. Into this tangled story of the murder of a small Russian landowner and the subsequent trial of Dmitry, one of his three sons, are interwoven the profound questions of the existence of God, morality and human freedom.

Dmitry Karamazov, a man of loose morals and high passions, appears to be guilty of the horrible crime of parricide. The murdered father, Fyodor, both hated and feared Dmitry. The two had quarreled over money countless times. Moreover, it was known to everyone that both men were madly in love with the same woman, Grushenka, whom the old man was tempting to become his mistress with three thousand rubles. This money Dmitry regarded as his by rights, and *he* needed this very sum to win Grushenka's favor.

When the old man is found murdered and robbed of his three thousand rubles, suspicion falls on Dmitry. The evidence is weighty. At the time of the murder he is seen running away from his father's home by a servant whom he knocks unconscious in his flight. Afterwards he is seen running through town, at a civil servant's home, and at a merchant's store, with blood-stained hands and coat, clutching a large bundle of rubles in his hand. He is apprehended at the height of a wild orgy with Grushenka, spending and drinking freely, though it is well known that the day before he had been penniless.

But Dmitry is innocent of the murder of his father. Though he had the opportunity and motive —indeed, he felt an overwhelming desire to do away with his hated rival—at the last minute he could not go through with the terrible deed. Why? He can give no reason except that "God was watching over me then." This coarse, sensual man was stayed by a power beyond him.

The real murderer is Smerdyakov, the crafty, twisted epileptic servant of the murdered man. But though Smerdyakov actually killed Fyodor, the servant believes that the guilt of the crime rests equally on Ivan, Dmitry's brother. Ivan is a sharp contrast to Dmitry. He is an intellectual, not a sensualist, a man with revolutionary ideas who professes not to believe in God. During the trial of Dmitry, Ivan goes to see Smerdyakov and is confronted with the brutal truth about his father's murder.

Smerdyakov tells Ivan that Ivan himself is guilty, partly because Ivan wished his father killed and made it plain that he would not inform on the murderer. But there is an even more profound reason for Ivan's guilt. Smerdyakov tells Ivan that it is from him that he learned that there is no such thing as morality, and therefore that it was "all right" to kill the old man. Ivan begs to know how the murder occurred and whether his brother Dmitry was involved:

Listen, did you kill him alone? With or without my brother?

Only with you, sir. I killed him with your help, sir. Your brother's quite innocent, sir.

All right, all right. We'll talk about me,

> later. Why do I keep on trembling? Can't utter a word.
>
> You was brave enough then, sir. Everything, you said, is permitted, and look how frightened you are now![1]

Ivan's words have come back to roost. Everything is permitted! And why is everything permitted? Smerdyakov answers this question as well.

> ... That was just a dream, sir, and mostly because "everything is permitted." This you did teach me, sir, for you talked to me a lot about such things: for if there's no everlasting God, there's no such thing as virtue, and there's no need of it at all. Yes, sir, you were right about that. That's the way I reasoned.[2]

If there is no God, there is no such thing as right and wrong; there is no need for morality.

According to Ivan's former way of thinking, there is neither God nor immortality, and the man who knows this, the new man, has the right to become a "man-god." To this new man, though he be the only one in the whole world, "everything is permitted." There is no law for God, and the man-god may "lightheartedly jump over every barrier of the old moral code of the former man-slave."[3]

But Ivan (and Dostoevsky) cannot accept this world without good and evil. It is a nightmare world and at Dmitry's trial Ivan attempts to confess his own guilt and show who the real murderer is. Ivan, when confronted by his own guilt, is forced to acknowledge the reality of good and evil.

This is the dilemma posed by Dostoevsky. Is there a God? If so, there is a basis for morality. If not, then immorality and morality likewise perish. Dostoevsky believes in God, but that terrible "if" haunts him like a spectre: "If there is no God, then everything is permitted."

Albert Camus: Grappling with the Dilemma

This dilemma has been accepted by modern writers who lack Dostoevsky's resolute faith in God. Camus and Sartre live in the post-Christian world, in which God has been exiled and everything *is* permitted to man.

The novels and plays of Albert Camus, however, highlight this problem as no other writings of this century have. When Camus was awarded the Nobel Prize for literature in 1957, the official citation noted that he had earned the honor because of "his important literary production, which with clear-sighted earnestness illuminates the problems of the human conscience in our times." His struggles to hold on to morality in a world without God are highlighted in three novels: *The Stranger* (1942), *The Plague* (1948) and *The Fall* (1956). Here we see a man who is truly an existentialist, truly concerned with the meaning and problems of individual, concrete existence.

A. The Stranger: A Picture of Nihilism

The Stranger is a revealing picture of Monsieur Meursault, who is just that—a stranger. He is not a stranger in the ordinary sense that he lives among people who do not know him. Rather he is *the* stranger, the archetype of post-Christian man. He lives in the world in which God is absent and man is alienated, estranged. He is estranged from nature, from his fellow men and from himself. Throughout the novel Monsieur Meursault maintains a curious detachment from questions of morality or the meaning of existence. On the day of his mother's funeral he reveals how true a child of the post-Christian era he is. "So far as I knew, my mother, though not a professed atheist, had never given a thought to religion in her life."[4] From Meursault's earliest days, God had been absent. The life of Monsieur Meursault is a picture of Dostoevsky's nightmare come true. Here is a man who truly lives in the world in which "everything is permitted."

Meursault encounters two interesting persons. One is Salamano, an old man who takes his dog for a walk twice a day, a walk which always ends in a vicious beating, replete with vile curses and threats for the terror-stricken animal. This has gone on monotonously for eight years. The other person is Raymond, who is rumored to be a pimp and who is heartily disliked by all his neighbors except Meursault. Meursault apparently does not disapprove of any action, no matter how vile. His acceptance of these two shady figures is not an acceptance based on love which forgives their vices. From his vantage point there is nothing to forgive.

In one encounter Raymond tells Meursault that it is "a damned shame" the way Salamano treats his dog, and asks Meursault if he is not disgusted by Salamano's behavior. The answer is short and final. "No." He is not disgusted by the daily beating of a helpless animal. He simply has no reaction at all—no feelings of either approval or condemnation.

Similarly when Raymond brutally beats his former mistress, Meursault maintains a curiously detached attitude. The poor woman's piercing screams, described as making one's blood run cold, can be clearly heard by Meursault and by Meursault's mistress, Marie, who begs him to do something. Meursault describes the scene.

> Marie said, wasn't it horrible! I didn't answer
> anything. Then she asked me to go and fetch
> a policeman, but I told her I didn't like
> policemen.[5]

Afterwards Marie and Meursault sit down to lunch. She has lost her appetite as a result of the experience of hearing the beating, so Meursault "eats nearly all." He is as undisturbed by the beating of a human being as he was over the beating of a helpless dog.

Event follows event until the stranger commits a pointless murder. He shoots a man whom he doesn't even know, whom he has no real reason to kill. He shoots him, and then empties his gun, pumping four more shots into the victim's inert body. At no time during his interrogation or trial does Meursault show the slightest remorse. He is sorry for the deed only in the sense that he regrets his imprisonment, separation from Marie and eventual execution. He never shows any regret over his senseless taking of another man's life.

In prison, waiting for his execution, Meursault receives an unrequested visit from the chaplain. The chaplain enters and inquires as to why Meursault had not wanted him to come and visit him.

"Why," he asked, "don't you let me come to see you?"

I explained that I didn't believe in God.

"Are you really so sure of that?"

I said I saw no point in troubling my head about the matter, whether I believed or didn't was, to my mind, a question of little importance.[6]

The chaplain insists that Meursault could not be so sure about what he believes. Meursault replies only that he can at least be sure about what didn't interest him and that the question the chaplain had raised didn't interest him at all.

In *The Stranger* Camus has given us a masterful and realistic portrait of a man who lives in a world in which God is truly dead. There is only one thing wrong with this picture; it is simply not believable. As a character, Meursault is not convincing. By his consummate literary skill Camus almost pulls the trick off. The reader begins to empathize with Meursault; he almost comes alive. Almost. Then, just as the reader attains the empathy necessary to truly understand him, just as he begins to put himself in the place of the anti-hero, Meursault escapes him. The stranger remains a stranger. His actions are ultimately incomprehensible. A man with no conception at all of right and wrong, a man who has not the slightest interest in the question of whether death will be the end of it all, who could not care less about whether God exists, is simply inconceivable.

Possibly these qualities could be accepted in a psychotic, but Meursault seems to be a perfectly ordinary, sane little man. But has ever a man lived in Western culture who has not somewhere, sometime, in the stillness and darkness of the night, wondered whether or not God is really there? Has a man lived in Europe in the last 1,000 years who has not, when alone with himself, wondered if that final agony of death was really final? Did ever a man anywhere truly live who did not at some time evidence a belief in a moral order of some type, however different men's conceptions of morality have been? Can a man live without believing that some actions are right and some wrong, that everything is not permitted?

B. The Plague: The Struggle for Morality

Perhaps this was Camus' point. In any case the contrast between *The Stranger* and his next novel, *The Plague,* points up clearly the unreality of Meursault's world. Dr. Rieux, the central character of *The Plague,* is a living, breathing human, caught up in the thicket of life, concerned with the suffering of those around him.

Rieux is not the only realistic character in *The Plague.* Besides the doctor, there are a journalist, a civil servant, a criminal, a priest and a mysterious man of the world, Jean Tarrou. These men find themselves facing one of the most terrible of man's dread opponents, plague, in the dreary town of Oran, in North Africa. It is their reactions to the plague which illustrate so vividly the possible alternatives which face man in his moral plight.

The quarantined town of Oran soon acquires a deeper meaning. Completely cut off from the rest of the world, Oran becomes the world for its inhabitants. The plague which is raging within the walls of the city, causing untold suffering and death to thousands of innocent children as well as hardened sinners, represents the universal condition of mankind. We all face the plague. "Each of us has the plague within him; no one, no one on earth is free from it."[7]

And not only do we all face the plague, we all must do what we can to fight it. Though our efforts may be unsuccessful, indeed, though they be doomed to failure, each must do what he can to arrest the contagion.

Thus Camus is driven to affirming morality. There is a moral "ought." Man ought to do what he can to eliminate suffering, evil and oppression. But it is still a world without God. Camus simply cannot accept a world without morality. Even if there is no God, there *must* be right and wrong. It is an earnest attempt to extricate man from the horns of Dostoevsky's dilemma. The crucial question is how to retain morality in a world in which God is dead. This becomes explicit in a conversation between Rieux and Tarrou:

"It comes to this," Tarrou said almost casually; "What interests me is learning how to become a saint."

"But you don't believe in God."

"Exactly! Can one be a saint without God?—that's the problem, in fact, the only problem I'm up against today."[8]

Can one be a saint without believing in God? Tarrou's question is the question Camus himself believed to be the most important facing man. Essentially Camus is asking two things. *Is* there a moral order without God? Can anyone *be* moral— without God? Before answering these two questions let us first ask another question.

Why should a man choose to do good rather than evil? Camus feels that he can answer this question without reference to any divine "thou shalt." In essence, his answer is that no reason has to be given. The important thing is not to find *reasons* for being moral, but to *be* moral.

> For the moment I know this; there are sick people and they need curing. Later on, perhaps, they'll think things over; and so shall I. But what's wanted now is to make them well.[9]

There is a profound truth here. Man has some sort of intuitive knowledge that there is evil and that he must oppose it. This is a knowledge which goes so deep as to be unshaken by any philosophical arguments which attempt to show that "everything is permitted." It is an elemental conviction, a feeling about the nature of things.

> I only know that one must do what one can to cease being plague-stricken, and that's the only way in which we can hope for some peace, or failing that, a decent death.[10]

After having truly answered this question of why man should choose to do right by simply asserting that there is no reason (man just "ought to"), Camus is still left with his original two questions. Man asks not only why one should do right, but why some things *are* right. What is the basis of the moral order? Is God necessary? Camus answers only that there is no need to find a *reason* why right is right; it just is. We know the meaning of right and wrong, and hence have no need to discover a basis for that moral order.

But do we really *know* the moral order? Though
man is certainly aware *that* there is right and
wrong, and that he ought to do the right, is he
really so aware of what is right and what is wrong?
It is easy enough to agree in the abstract that men
ought to do good and not evil, but when the
situation gets concrete, sharp disagreement is the
rule rather than the exception.

And what about a Hitler? He believed he was
"right" in murdering millions of people. Unless we
know *why* some things are right, we will not truly
know *what* things are right. If there is no *reason*
why an action is wrong, no one will ever be able to
explain to any other human being why that action
was indeed wrong. Thus I can decide what is right
and what is wrong, but if someone disagrees with
me we have no common ground for discussion. If
he tells me that it is right to use other people to
increase one's own pleasure, I can merely say "You
are wrong." But then he could simply reply that I
was the one who was wrong. And suppose he had
the power to carry out his view of things? Suppose
he were a Hitler?

Camus seems to realize the problem of defining
morality. Having failed to find a *reason* for
morality, he is also unable to state clearly the
nature of man's moral obligation. He can only say
that it is a vague something, the nature of which
each person recognizes for himself. Rieux puts the
situation clearly in a conversation with Rambert,

the journalist:

> "There's no question of heroism in all this. It's a matter of common decency. That's an idea which may make some people smile, but the only means of fighting a plague is—common decency."
>
> "What do you mean by 'common decency'?" Rambert's tone was grave.
>
> "I don't know what it means for other people. But in my case I know that it consists in doing my job."[11]

It's just common decency! But what is common decency? Every man decides for himself, be he saint or sadist.

And even if this hurdle could be passed, there is another. In Camus' original question, "Can one be a saint without God?" there is another hidden question. Not only is he asking, "Is there morality without God?" but also, "Does man have the ability to do right without God's help?" Can man find the strength he needs to choose and to carry out the good within himself? It is here that we must cry with Camus, who fully realizes the desperate nature of the plight of post-Christian man. Tarrou is again Camus' mouthpiece:

> What's natural is the microbe. All the rest— health, integrity, purity (if you like)—is a product of the human will, of a vigilance that must never falter. . . . Yes, Rieux, it's a wearying business, being plague-stricken. . . . That's

> why everybody in the world looks so tired;
> everyone is more or less sick of the plague.
> But that is also why some of us, those who
> want to get the plague out of their systems,
> feel such desperate weariness, a weariness
> from which nothing remains to set us free ex-
> cept death.[12]

Victories over the plague are never lasting. We
struggle, but plague spells in the final analysis "a
never ending defeat."

C. The Fall: The Defeat of Man

This pessimism becomes still more evident in
Camus' third novel, *The Fall.* A man meets another
man in *Mexico City,* a shady little bar in Amster-
dam. This man spins out the story of his life, revealing that his eminently respectable past as a
Parisian lawyer who defended widows and orphans
had been only a veneer for his thoroughly corrupt
nature. This man testifies that his experience is the
universal lot of man.

> We cannot assert the innocence of anyone,
> whereas we can state with certainty the guilt
> of all. Every man testifies to the crime of all
> the others—that is my faith and hope.[13]

In *The Fall* we see Camus' disillusionment over the
possibility of morality in a world without God.
There is still a moral order. But there is no hope of
anyone ever being moral, of being truly good.

Camus seems finally to doubt whether he has

really discovered morality without God. The absolute freedom of a world where "everything is permitted" looms for him as it did for Dostoevsky, a nightmare. "At the end of all freedom is a court sentence; that's why freedom is too heavy to bear."[14] At the conclusion of *The Fall* the narrator of the story comes to the conclusion that man must choose a God-substitute in order to exist. Even slavery is preferable to the awful world where man is alone. Slavery, in fact, is the only definitive solution.

> Ah, *mon cher,* for anyone who is alone, without God and without a master, the weight of days is dreadful. Hence one must choose a master, God being out of style.[15]

Struggling all his life with Dostoevsky's dilemma, Camus has shown himself to be a man with a deeply engrained moral sense. He refuses to admit that everything is permitted, and searches vainly for a way to become a saint without believing in God. In a world where "God is out of style" Camus becomes for us a prophet of despair. Despair lies just beneath the surface in all three of these novels, a melancholy undertone to Camus' affirmation of morality.

Despair and the Existential Necessity of Morality

What is the nature of this despair? Perhaps Camus' despair can be seen as a despair which points beyond itself. In the depths of despair, unable to

understand the why or how of life, Camus shouts
that this is a world where each of us *must* do what
he can to fight plague. The apparent loss of morality which follows the death of God moves Camus
to affirm the necessity of morality in a passionate
and dogmatic manner. Just as a man may be unconscious of the air he breathes until he is thrust
into an alien and suffocating atmosphere, so the
man who despairs of morality may come to realize
its necessity. The threat of the loss of good and evil
compels man to affirm the reality of good and evil.
In a world where choice is pointless, where right
and wrong are illusions, hope is an alien. The affirmation of morality posits the seeds of hope, stir-
ring but not yet thrusting upward through the en-
crusted ground.

Behind these seeds of hope lies the feeling that
right and wrong are not optional luxuries for man,
but are ultimate and basic. No creed or philosophy
which fails to account for this can truly be adequate, when tested in the court of human existence. A materialism or naturalism which merely
accounts for why men have moral notions simply
will not account for morality. Such theories, instead of explaining why something *is* right, merely
explain why men believe something is right.
Theories which hold that right and wrong are ra-
tionalizations of pleasure, or projections of child-
hood fears, or which explain morality as the result
of the fact that animals which had these peculiar

notions that some things were "right" and others "wrong" were best fitted for evolutionary survival, will inevitably destroy morality and lead to despair.

As soon as I am told that right and wrong are my creations, rooted in my subconscious, or explainable in terms of physiological processes in the brain—in short, that the whole business of morals can be given a perfectly natural, scientific explanation—then I simultaneously become aware that right and wrong have no objective validity.

The essence of morality is an objective "ought," which is completely independent of my wishes, desires or fears. Only from this "ought" can come the call of conscience which can compel a man to say, "Here I stand, I can do no other."

If a white man believes that he ought to treat a black man as a man, he believes that this is the right action. He believes that hate and bigotry are *wrong*, regardless of the fact that he may live in a racist society where discrimination is regarded as "all right." If his belief can be completely explained as a result of a certain feeling of benevolence for blacks that he possesses which most white people in his society do not possess, then the moral issue is dissipated. So one feels one way toward blacks, and another feels another way. On this basis, how can any man argue that the beliefs which his feelings give rise to are right, and certain others wrong?

Some men like bananas and others do not, but from this fact no moral judgment can be drawn. To take a stand against racial prejudice, one must affirm that something is right, namely treating every man as a man, regardless of the feelings or beliefs that *anyone* may have. An ethical demand is an obligation laid upon a man; if that obligation is explained away, then the ethical demand is spurious.

Certainly men have moral notions, and very often (if not always) psychological or physiological explanations of how men come to have these notions can be given. But such explanations cannot explain the validity of such notions. Unless in some cases men's moral beliefs correspond with a state of affairs in objective reality, then there can be no moral order. Everything is permitted. To retain a moral order, I must be aware that some things *are* right and other things *are* wrong, not that I have strange feelings that some things are right and others wrong. The attempt to give a naturalistic explanation of the origin of the moral "ought" is merely an attempt to explain away the validity of that "ought." The ethical "ought" is a regulative principle, which, if explained as a human construction, becomes an illusion. If it is an illusion, man is constantly deceived into believing that something in the nature of reality makes an objective demand upon him.

Despair swiftly follows the discovery that morality is illusory. Life becomes a deceiver, thrusting upon man spurious choices, sending him illusions of responsibility and guilt. In such a world no true moral judgment can be made, even upon a Hitler. Hitler's moral notions merely differed from most people's. Surely the psychologist or biologist could give an account of why he happened to feel the way he did, just as an account can be given of why the majority of men feel Hitler was "evil." All such beliefs are merely naturalistic "facts." From the naturalistic standpoint, how could anyone say that Hitler was truly responsible for his beliefs and actions? Responsible for what? Responsible to whom? Presumably, Hitler was not responsible for the natural physical laws which might be thought to have produced him and his odious beliefs.

If morality can be naturalistically explained, then moralists should feel no pride in their espousal of brotherhood, love or justice. It just happened that they believed these things to be "right." From a strict scientific standpoint, as value-beliefs they are on the same plane with the espousal of robbery, injustice and murder. No true argument can be given that love, brotherhood and justice *are* right, unless some things are *right*.

In this post-Christian era Camus has plumbed the depths of despair. But even his despair includes an affirmation, a leap of faith as it were. Camus demonstrates that right and wrong possess a "gut" reality which cannot be explained away. Every man who goes on living, making moral choices and defending those choices, affirms by his deeds, if not his theories, that there is a moral order. Without this affirmation it is doubtful whether any individual could survive, and it is certain that community would perish.

If in despair we learn that some acts are right, then despair does not lead to nihilism. Despair points beyond itself. There is even a vague hope—perhaps not yet a hope but only a feeling—that if the how and why of morality could be given, then the road to hope would be illuminated. Perhaps an exploration of right and wrong will yield an understanding of the universe and man's situation which goes far deeper than the predictive laws of physical science. Thus, in our journey through the valley of despair we encounter evidence, however tenuous that evidence may be, that despair is not a dead end to which man is inevitably driven, but is in some cases the prelude to a fuller understanding of human existence, a realistic understanding that nevertheless at least lends hope that there is a pathway to hope.

Yet Camus, despite his affirmation of morality, did not travel that pathway. To the contrary, he became increasingly pessimistic in his writings. Why? Because Camus honestly faces another consequence of a world which includes a moral order. In such a world man faces, Camus realized, "a court sentence."

A world in which some actions are "right" and some things are "good" seems to be a world in which hope could flourish, a vast improvement over a world in which there are no reasons for any ethical decision. But Camus clearly sees that man, though aware of the existence of the moral order, is free to choose as he wills. Without worrying about the numberless cases where a man may be unaware that his actions are wrong, it is evident enough that every man, on certain occasions, chooses to act in a manner which he knows in his innermost being to be wrong, regardless of how he may rationalize the action to others. In such a world where every man testifies to the corrupt nature of every other, the unconditional moral obligation felt by man is a judgment, a threatening court sentence. Looking upon the reality of human existence, Camus concluded that there is no hope of anyone being truly moral.

Thus something else seems necessary, and I know no better word for it than *grace*. Where can post-Christian man look for grace? Where can he find the forgiveness that will enable him to accept himself as he is and to commune with his fellow man? It is plain that true hope will require nothing less. What is the relationship of this forgiveness man needs to the moral obligations he feels? If man's moral experience is to engender hope, perhaps he will require what Camus could not find: an explanation of the how and why of the moral order.

the
despair
of
meaning

chapter 3

Before continuing our exploration of moral values, we must continue our journey through the valley of despair, looking for other catalysts to hope. The despair of morality robbed human ethical decisions of their meaning. But there is also a deep despair which robs every human choice of its point. This is the despair of meaning.

The Question of Suicide

Meaninglessness is a close companion to the despair of morality. *Meaninglessness* is a vague word and it implies different things to different people. But it usually includes as a bare minimum the "absence of purpose." As there is no reason for morality in the post-Christian world, so there is no reason for living. As Camus says in *The Myth of Sisyphus,* the only truly significant philosophical question is suicide. Why should I not snuff out my life? Why should I make the effort to go on living? This is the most urgent of all questions, philosophical, scientific or ethical. If it cannot be answered, no other question can even be asked.

Is this a necessary question? It is certainly not necessary in the sense that everyone asks it. Quite the contrary, most people struggle through life without ever asking it. They just go on living, without feeling they must find a reason to live, a justification for their existence. But not everyone.

Some men do not "just go on living." A few men, every day in some obscure corner of the world, end their lives by their own choice. And how many go on living, not because they have a reason for living, but because they are afraid to die?

We have seen that every honest thinker who is truly grappling with the meaning of his own existence must face the reality of death. He is going to die anyway. In view of this, is life absurd? Is there any purpose in prolonging life, any reason why living is superior to dying?

Sartre and Camus: Grappling with Meaninglessness

This problem of meaninglessness is at the very heart of the thinking of Jean Paul Sartre. Sartre discusses it in terms of *essence* and *existence.* Does man have an essence, a reason for being, or purpose for existing? Or is man simply bare existence, a being who first of all just *is*, and is something only after that?

According to Sartre, if man were a creation of God then his essence would precede his existence. A builder who builds a house must first have an idea or plan for that house. Similarly, God must have had an idea of what man was intended to be before he created him. This idea would be man's essence, or what man was intended to be. Man's purpose in life would be to actualize this essence or purpose completely, to become what he had been intended to be. But Sartre says this is not the case.

Man has no essence. There is no *reason* why man exists. He just does. *That* he is precedes *what* he is. If a man asks, "Who am I?" Sartre answers, "You are nothing but bare existence." And this existence is a meaningless existence. The anti-hero of Sartre's first novel, *Nausea,* describes the character of this existence perfectly.

> Nothing happens while you live. The scenery changes, people come in and go out, that's all. There are no beginnings. Days are tacked on to days without rhyme or reason, an inter-minable, monotonous addition.[1]

Life is a meaningless series of disconnected events. This is so because there is no purpose for man, nothing significant for him to accomplish or to be.

"I was just thinking," I tell him laughing, "that here we sit, all of us, eating and drinking to preserve our precious existence, and really there is nothing, nothing, absolutely no reason for existing."[2]

Before attempting a detailed description of this meaningless, absurd world, it would be well to try to understand how and why Sartre and Camus have been driven to this conclusion. It is paradoxical that their world should be devoid of meaning, because from one point of view their whole philosophy can be characterized as an attempt to reinject meaning into the world.

Sartre and practically all other existentialist writers are in conscious reaction to the world in which science has become God and man an adjunct of technology. The Christian existentialist, such as Marcel, shares this concern with Sartre, Camus and Heidegger. Gabriel Marcel protests in his essay "On the Ontological Mystery" against the reduction of man to "a conglomeration of functions." The life, loves and death of a man cannot be reduced to that pseudo-scientific category of the "purely natural."

Karl Jaspers, in *Man in the Modern Age,* similarly protests against a world in which man is a thing, a cog in a vast machine. Sartre concurs in this protest. He explicitly rejects determinism, as represented by Marx, Freud or any other thinker who denies man's freedom, as destructive of meaning. Man is not determined by economic forces or by irrational, subconscious desires. He is free. Man is not merely an organ stop or a piano key. He is a conscious being, and to say that he is conscious amounts to saying that he is free.

But though Sartre and Camus see clearly the sterility of life in the twentieth century, they have no means of enriching that life. They lay bare the meaningless character of a world in which technology is supreme, but they are powerless to reinject meaning into that world. Still, they try.

Sartre attempts to see in man's freedom the means of finding meaning, and Camus attempts to find the meaning of life in its very absurdity. But these attempts are unconvincing. They have the desperate ring of a drowning man trying to hold on to the water which slips around and through his fingers.

Sartre attempts to reinject meaning into man's world by absolutizing human freedom. In Sartre's world the God whom he sees as the necessary author of any objective meaning is dead. Feeling the need for a successor, Sartre lights upon man himself as the only available candidate. Man becomes God. Whatever values exist are created by man.

If man unthinkingly accepts the values of his culture as objectively valid, he is in the state of "bad faith," the self-deception which makes it possible for normal life to go on. The authentic man creates his own values *ex nihilo*. That is, he chooses them for himself, accepting full responsibility for his choice yet completely aware that there is nothing in the nature of things to govern his decision. His choice is completely isolated and of necessity bars communication and dialogue. A choice made without reasons is a choice which cannot be explained.

How can Sartrean freedom provide meaning for man? If there are no *significant* choices, no *reasons* to choose one option over another, then of what value is the freedom to choose? Unless there is some goal towards which man may exercise his freedom, it is a meaningless freedom. He can choose, but the choice is absurd. Sartrean freedom is only "freedom-from," not true freedom, which is "freedom-to."

In *The Myth of Sisyphus* Camus urges a similar tack. Sartre had urged that man could find meaning via an absurd choice. Camus argues that man can find justification for living by choosing to accept the absurdity of the whole situation in which man finds himself.

> The absurd man . . . catches sight of a burning and frigid, transparent and limited universe in which nothing is possible but everything is given, and beyond which all is collapse and nothingness. He can then decide to accept such a universe and draw from it his strength, his refusal to hope, and the unyielding evidence of a life without consolation.[3]

It is undoubtedly courageous to affirm life when there is no meaning, to go on living without hope or consolation, but this is not a solution to the problem of finding meaning. It is rather an evasion. Camus asks us just to accept somehow this absurd universe, to make an arbitrary, indeed absurd, act of the will. But this is not an answer, only a resolution to quit seeking an answer.

Sartre and Camus both feel keenly the loss of meaning in the world, but they fail to provide any basis for that meaning. They protest against the lowering of man to an object, but they have no means to make him truly human, nor even any concept of what it *means* to be truly human. In their reaction to the technological world which has made man a thing, they have, to use Sartre's own terminology, made man a "no-thing," bare existence which is really nothing at all.

Nausea: The Repulsiveness of a Meaningless World

Sartre gives a powerful and moving description of a world devoid of meaning or purpose in *Nausea*. This work gives a picture of Antoine Roquentin, who has become an archetype of the existentialist man. Here is a post-Christian man, for whom God is dead, a man who takes despair as the measure of life.

Roquentin is an adventurer, world traveler and scholar who has settled in the provincial town of Bouville, France, to conclude a historical work on the life of the Marquis de Rollebon. In the midst of his research he comes to realize the meaninglessness of his life.

A powerful consciousness of the nothingness within himself and in the world around him fills Roquentin with the *nausea*. Existence is ugly, bare and futile. The world is obscene. Man is that creature who demands a reason for being, and yet is confronted only by an inhuman, brute world which offers no explanation either for itself or for man. Man's existence in such a world constitutes the absurd. Roquentin describes the nature of human existence as a wheel of purposeless activity.

Roquentin makes a series of desperate attempts to find objective meaning and escape the nausea. His search leads him through every alternative which seems open to post-Christian man—every alternative, that is, except the religious, which he believes science has relegated to the Dark Ages.

A. Searching for Truth

First, Roquentin looks to *science* itself. As a scholar he has his work. Perhaps historical science will be his salvation. But Roquentin comes to realize the illusory nature of knowledge. The unity and order, the intelligibility he seems to discover in the world, is not really discovered. Rather he comes to see that he has invented it. His work on the Marquis de Rollebon illustrates this.

I am beginning to believe that nothing can

ever be proved. There are honest hypotheses which take the facts into account: but I sense so definitely that they come from me, and that they are simply a way of unifying my own knowledge. Not a glimmer comes from Rollebon's side.[4]

Historical knowledge in this case is a paradigm of knowledge generally. Knowledge fails to give man meaning, because knowledge is a subjective creation (projection, really) of man. Roquentin discovers that there is a point at which scientific explanation fails, if science is regarded as that which is to give the meaning and rationale for man's existence.

Camus is also aware of the inadequacy of science to provide man an understanding of his world and his place in it, and has described this failure even more powerfully.

Yet all the knowledge on earth will give me nothing to assure me that this world is mine. You describe it to me and you teach me to classify it. You enumerate its laws and in my thirst for knowledge I admit that they are true. You take apart its mechanism and my hope increases. At the final stage you teach me that this wondrous and multi-colored universe can be reduced to the atom and that the atom itself can be reduced to the electron. All this is good and I wait for you to continue. But you tell me of an invisible planetary system in which electrons gravitate around a nucleus. You explain this world to me with an image. I realize then that you have been reduced to poetry: I shall never know. Have I the time to become indignant? You have already changed theories. So that science that was to teach me everything ends up in a metaphor, that uncertainty is resolved in a work of art. What need had I of so many efforts? The soft lines of these hills and the hand of evening on this troubled heart teach me much more.[5]

The failure of scientific knowledge to satisfy Roquentin's existential anguish was foreordained. Man has been forced to recognize that the task assigned to science by optimistic humanists like John Dewey lies far beyond its scope. Science can no more provide a reason for existing than it can provide a basis for the moral "ought."

Man does not exist for science, but science for man. It is now clearly evident that the impact of science on human existence may be either good or evil, a boon or a curse, depending on the wisdom and values held by those who wield the sword of technology, or who pen social ideas, which in some cases are indeed mightier than the sword.

Science is powerless to resolve the dilemma of human existence. If a scientist could give a complete, mechanistic explanation of man, if he could construct an empirical cause and effect chain which could explain all human activity in terms of electrons, protons, etc., would man have any better understanding of what it means to be truly human? Would the fact that man is *conscious* of what goes on around him, that he *questions* why he is here, that he marvels at the intricacies he discovers in nature, be more explicable? In fact, a scientific account of man and his world, if seriously believed to be an account of the way things *really are* in their innermost being, far from making sense of man and his world, destroys the meaning of every human activity, including science.

The scientist is a man, too. If the task of the scientist be taken as somehow to show that the world of sounds, colors, morality, etc., is illusory and that the "true" world is a world of masses and volumes, velocities and accelerations, forces and charges, then that task is self-defeating. Insofar as a scientist wishes his theories to be *understood,* and not to remain abstract mathematical equations and formulas which enable us to predict future behavior, he must state his theory in language. However sharply modified his language may be, it ultimately derives its meaning from the ordinary world of conscious experience. The meaning of solidity is derived from ordinary, conscious experience of tables and stones. The meaningfulness of scientific theories is dependent on the validity of man's everyday experience of the people and world around him.

The scientist eats, drinks, plays bridge, makes love to his wife or mistress and ultimately dies, just as other men do. When facing his own death, he must question the meaning of all his activities, including the meaning of science itself. If no answer can be given to these questions, then science, far from delivering man from the despair of meaning, is wholly engulfed by this despair.

B. Searching for Thrills

Sartre's anti-hero, Roquentin, having failed to justify his existence in scholarly endeavor, turns to another area, far removed from the test tube and the library. Perhaps meaning can be found in *experiences,* in the thrill and excitement of adventure. Turning from knowledge and reflection, Roquentin examines events experienced in their immediacy. This is the Ernest Hemingway life, the man of action. Roquentin has lived an adventurous life in the ordinary sense of the word. Is it possible to find the meaning of life in *experiences,* be they of pain or pleasure, beauty or ugliness, danger or boredom?

Roquentin has traveled through Central Europe, North Africa and the Far East. He has seen and done many things which the average man only dreams of. Yet he fails to find meaning in his experiences. In fact, when seen clearly there is no possibility of having any true "adventures."

I have never had adventures. Things have hap-

pened to me, events, incidents, anything you
like. But no adventures. It isn't a question of
words; I am beginning to understand.[6]

To understand what? Roquentin is beginning to
understand the true character of experience. An
adventure has no objective reality. Events simply
happen. They do not mean anything. The feeling
of adventure arises from the way *I* link these events
together, as if they had some purpose or one thing
"led to another." But this feeling is a subjective
creation. Man, the creature who desires meaning,
who must have it at all costs, projects meaning
upon the world. But it is not really there. What is
there is only bare existence and the absurdity of
man's presence in such a world.

Sartre is correct in his observation that events in
their immediacy are not adventures. Only when
events are invested with meaning is there true adventure. When the existence of something worthwhile and meaningful, such as a human life, is
threatened, then there are dangers and thrills.
When two people deeply in love succeed in overcoming an obstacle, there is joy and happiness.
When a man demonstrates courage and strength by
accomplishing the significant feat of climbing a
mountain, there is satisfaction.

The meaning of these events is derived not from
the events alone, but from the web of human relationships and actions which enclose the event. To
the man in despair, who sees no point to his own

existence nor to any of his actions, adventures cannot be meaningful. The search for adventure is merely another feeble attempt to project the illusion of meaning on something external. If man could persuade himself that this something possesses a "hard" validity, then perhaps he could build his life around that something.

Roquentin sees clearly that adventures, thrills and moods alone cannot provide man with a meaningful world. The human element is too pervasive. Just as the validity of science is dependent on human activities (interpretive hypotheses, deductive reasoning, conscious activity in general), so the meaning of adventures presupposes the meaningfulness of the human activities which create "adventures." If there is no value or significance to human existence, there can be none attached to human adventures.

C. Searching for a Cause: Humanism

The third possibility which Sartre offers for our perusal in *Nausea* is *rational humanism*. This is personified in "The Self-Taught Man," a friend of Roquentin in Bouville. This gentle man is educating himself by reading through all the books of the Bouville Library—in alphabetical order! The Self-Taught Man, in a touching passage, tries to communicate his "faith" in humanism, which seems to provide his life with meaning. "There is a goal, Monsieur, there is a goal. . . . there is humanity."[7]

Yes, there are people. But Roquentin knows only too well what people are like. Selfish, bigoted, ugly, the humanists are no different. The radical humanist, the Communist humanist, the liberal humanist, the humanist philosopher do not really love men or each other:

> They all hate each other: as individuals, naturally not as men. But the Self-Taught Man doesn't know it; he has locked them up inside himself like cats in a bag and they are tearing each other in pieces without his noticing it.[8]

It is quite easy to love mankind, quite impossible to love individual people. And why should one? Roquentin, who is an atheist, in a strange passage chides the Self-Taught Man for his lack of belief in God, which would provide the only possible basis for a true humanism. To be a humanist, one must believe in a God who guarantees that people are worth loving.

> "I know," I [Roquentin] tell him [the Self-Taught Man], "I know that all men are admirable. You are admirable. I am admirable. In as far as we are creations of God, naturally."[9]

The Self-Taught Man thinks that Roquentin is kidding him, but Roquentin's thoughts reveal how serious he is. "Without realizing it, he [the Self-Taught Man] has abandoned the love of men in Christ."[10]

The collapse of rational humanism comes finally in a scene of almost comic pathos. The Self-Taught Man, reading at the library, is caught stroking the hand of a small boy, whispering softly in his ear. The emptiness and superficial nature of his commitment to "mankind" stands out in clear contrast to the virility of human depravity. The Self-Taught Man "loves" little boys more than he loves mankind.

No more powerful description could be given of the failure of naturalistic humanism, unless that description be taken from the history of the Third Reich. If history has taught man anything, it is that man can be expected to act in the most inhuman way possible, regardless of the degree of education, culture and sophistication. That Germany produced Goethe and Beethoven as well as Hitler does not refute this hypothesis. It only demonstrates that barbarities will occur wherever there are men, whether the place be Biafra, Viet Nam or the streets of Chicago.

Humanism is only possible on the premise that man is indeed significant and possesses intrinsic worth. It therefore presupposes that human existence is meaningful; it cannot *make* human existence meaningful. If there is a "point" to life, if there is a reason for man to go on living, significant tasks for man to accomplish, objective truths for man to know, challenging experiences for man to undergo, then humanism makes sense. But before embarking on a program to improve man's lot, it would be well to first attain an understanding of that lot, and what an improvement of it would be.

A mere affirmation of humanism, apart from an understanding of man's existential plight, does not ensure meaning. Rather, such an affirmation of humanism, like the situation of the Self-Taught Man, includes an element of the comic. It conjures up the vision of a group of men, each living for the sake of other men, without any understanding of why they should live for others, or why *any* man should *live* at all. It also conjures up the sad image of men who love mankind but despise their neighbor, of organizers of charities who dislike the poor and of self-proclaimed liberators who enslave their fellow man.

D. Searching for Love

Having failed to find a reason to live in science, experience or humanism, Roquentin finally turns to that panacea of modern man—*love,* particularly sexual love. But mere sex is certainly not the answer. To satisfy his urges Roquentin goes fairly regularly to see Francoise, a woman who runs a cafe. But sex is not meaningful. It is mechanical, dull; they hardly speak. Roquentin is well aware how quickly the mad passion of sex gives way to boredom when unaccompanied by significant personal encounter. It is not just to sex that Roquentin looks. Rather he hopes to find love, real love.

All through the novel his thoughts go back to Anny, his former mistress. Anny is clearly his last hope.

Roquentin receives a note from Anny, the first communication he has had from her in years, and he makes plans to go to see her. But Roquentin's mounting excitement does not disguise from the reader the inevitability of his defeat. He arrives and after a few minutes of superficial conversation, Roquentin realizes that they have nothing to share; love is an impossibility. "Anny is sitting opposite to me, we haven't seen each other for four years and we have nothing to say."[11]

That Roquentin concludes that love is incapable of providing meaning for man is not surprising in view of Sartre's analysis of love in his other works, particularly *Being and Nothingness*. The aim of love is merely to appropriate the freedom of the other, to make oneself the object of the lover's will. The lover wishes to "capture a consciousness."[12] The picture of love as an unselfish giving of oneself is denounced as a myth. Sartre apparently does not believe that true giving of oneself is possible. "To give is to appropriate by destruction while utilizing this destruction to enslave another."[13] Man is completely egoistic. He loves only to enslave his lover; he gives only to destroy the recipient of the gift.

This is a profound description of love in a meaningless world. Each person, knowing deep down that he is truly nothing, desperately seeks to attain some kind of "status" in the eyes of others. In such diverse phenomena as racism and "keeping up with the Joneses" each man is engaged in a struggle to extract from others the recognition that he is "somebody." The more a man feels he really is nobody, the more he craves this esteem in the eyes of others. Even man's unselfish acts are really designed to prove that he is "better" than other, more egotistical souls. In love, this attempt to make oneself something at the expense of others is most insidious.

In a world without meaning, where man is nothing, love can be nothing else but this desire to degrade another. Love cannot be genuine giving, sharing and communion, if man possesses nothing of value to give or to share. If a man cannot stand himself, he will certainly not reverence his lover. Each lover will strive pitifully to extract from his lover a recognition, a proof that he is somebody.

The tragedy is that this can be achieved only through enslavement. Insofar as I can ensure that you exist only for me, that your every word and deed is for my benefit, I am redeemed. If I am successful in robbing my lover of whatever value she possesses, I appropriate that value. The irony is that such a relationship destroys what *is* of real value in a person.

The despair of love is true despair. The horror of Roquentin's world is now fully clear. The nausea is overwhelming.

E. Nausea's Conclusion: Man Is Superfluous

Roquentin has failed to discover meaning in anything outside himself. Everywhere he seeks meaning, he must first untie the Gordian knot of his *own* meaning. The root of despair is the meaningless character of human existence. And Roquentin's own existence seems to be completely precarious. He can never find that reason for living which he seeks within himself. His own existence is radically contingent; there is no reason behind it.

Roquentin recognizes that he has no right to exist, but just appeared by chance.[14] Man is gratuitous, superfluous, *de trop.* The only relationship he can establish between himself and the things around him is that of being *In the way.*

I dreamed vaguely of killing myself to wipe out at least one of these superfluous lives. But even my death would have been *In the way. In the way,* my corpse, my blood on these stones, between those plants, at the back of this smiling garden. And the decomposed flesh would have been *In the way* in the earth which would receive my bones, at last, cleaned, stripped, peeled, proper and clean as teeth, it would have been *In the way;* I was *In the way* for eternity. [15]

The Unreality of Sartre's World

Nausea is a unique novel. It gives a powerful and

convincing description of a world in which life is meaningless, in which existence is nauseating. It pictures the despair which ought to follow the recognition that life has no meaning, structure, order or significance to give man a "place" in the overall order of things. However there is one thing that Sartre must reckon with, and that is that human activities often *seem* to be meaningful.

Even simple, everyday activities, such as a handshake, seem charged with meaning. As Thomas Howard has convincingly shown in his book, *An Antique Drum,* humans, all of us, behave *as if* our activities had meaning. From such simple occasions as a noon meal to the solemnity of a state funeral, men clothe their activities with form and ritual to recognize and emphasize the importance of what they are doing. Though from these particles alone no overall framework can be grasped, they do seem to be clues or pointers, evidences of meaning. If the world is truly devoid of meaning, all these evidences are merely trappings, illusions of meaning. But they are there and must be explained, even if they are illusions. Things *seem* to happen as if they were related to other things, as if one thing *meant* another. Life does not seem at first glance to be the series of meaningless, disconnected events which Roquentin proclaims it to be.

Sartre deals with the apparent meaning of human existence by looking at the artistic medium which recreates human existence, that of fiction.

In a very revealing passage Sartre gives a unique analysis of the nature of fiction or storytelling, or at least non-existentialist fiction. (Presumably his own novels do not fit this description.)

According to Sartre, fiction does not give a true picture of life. Living is a meaningless round of events, but in novels, biographies and stories there is often created an illusion of purpose.

> That's living [meaninglessness]. But everything changes when you tell about life; it's a change no one notices: the proof is that people talk about true stories. As if there could possibly be true stories; things happen one way and we tell about them in the opposite sense.[16]

In the story, the end is there at the beginning, transforming all the seemingly irrelevant details. The reader knows that the author did not point out the emptiness of the street and the noise of the creaking door for no reason. The significance of these facts will be evident later on. But in life there is no "end" towards which the action moves. Fiction is a lie.

Sartre is forced to say this about literature. If life has no meaning, then it is impossible for art to communicate that meaning. But art does communicate meaning, and Sartre is forced to dismiss this as illusion. It is precisely the nature of art to communicate the artist's vision of reality. And if this vision of reality did not contain an element of

truth, universal truth, the work would never be
recognized as a classic, transcending a particular
time or place. The reader of Dostoevsky's *The
Brothers Karamazov* sees in that work something
of himself and the world about him. The work
rings true. The greatness of this novel consists precisely in the power of this vision. It compels the
reader's assent. He must acknowledge that a slice
of his own existential predicament is contained in
the gripping story.

By contrast *Nausea* is not great art. Sartre is a
masterful writer and there are many great passages,
but ultimately Roquentin is no more believable a
character than Camus' Meursault. Roquentin's
metaphysical anguish seems somehow contrived.
He is not a man whose sensibilities are such that he
experiences what every man experiences, only to a
more acute degree. Rather, he seems unable to feel
and experience as most men. His anguish seems
exceptional, the result of a defect in his personality
rather than a heightened sensitivity.

Existential Choices and Metaphysical Beliefs

We are here calling Sartrean despair into question.
The despair of Roquentin is not the despair which
will lead to hope. Sartrean despair points nowhere,
leads only to nothingness and the absurd.

It is precisely because it leads to meaninglessness
that we must question this despair. Is Sartrean despair the universal despair which is encountered by

any honest thinker who seriously considers the meaning of his existence in view of his own death? Or is this despair inauthentic, exceptional, perhaps even pathological?

The despair we have been examining is primarily a metaphysical stance, a fundamental attitude toward reality. Perhaps it is fair to call such a stance a metaphysical belief, as it clearly presupposes certain beliefs about man and the kind of world man finds himself in, specifically a belief that the world is objectively meaningless.

Now it is a peculiar characteristic of beliefs of this kind that they can never be *proved* to be true. As many have pointed out, after 2,500 years of disputes, philosophers seem no closer to agreement than in the days of Plato and Democritus. This suggests strongly that philosophical beliefs, particularly those we have called metaphysical, differ somehow from scientific hypotheses or mathematical theorems. There seem to be no facts which can *conclusively* decide metaphysical questions, no experiments which can be performed, no proofs which can be constructed to finally decide the matter. Yet the issues at stake are important enough for the world's greatest thinkers to passionately disagree over their answers for more than 2,500 years.

It seems clear that a man does not choose a metaphysical belief by simply adding up the facts on both sides and picking the most reasonable alternative. There are many factors at work which help to determine the fundamental governing attitude of a man's life. I am sure a Freudian or Marxist could easily provide us with some of these factors. Theologians and philosophers could no doubt point to others. Without denying that man feels an obligation to be intellectually honest, it can easily be seen that the adoption of a fundamental belief about the nature of reality is not made at the end of a Q.E.D. mathematical proof but is the result of an existential *choice.*

Such a choice may be unconscious, but it is clear that in some sense every man makes such a choice and that his decision must truly be one that he can live with. We thus see despair as closely connected with choosing. Though we speak of despair as a state (he languished in despair), it is plain that man may *choose* to despair or to hope. This is evidenced by Sartre and Marcel who, confronted by the same world, choose these different options.

The question which now arises is which of these two alternatives is *more* honest to the facts of our existence. When Sartre declares the world is meaningless, he is purporting to describe a state of affairs. To assert that the world is meaningless is to assert that no overall pattern or framework exists, that things (including man) just *are.* They are not *for something,* and they do not *mean* anything. When Sartre describes the world in this way, he is telling us what he sees.

What we must determine is whether or not Sartre's despair logically precedes or follows his description of the world as meaningless. Has he looked at the world, seen its absurdity and as a consequence been forced to despair of finding any meaning? Or has he *chosen* (existentially) to despair and, as a consequence of his despair, looked at the world and seen only absurdity and nothingness?

The evidence shows, I think, that Sartre's choice of despair is, like other metaphysical stances, the result of an existential decision. Thus, his despair antedates the discovery of meaninglessness. His "report" as to the nature of human experience is conditioned by his own despair.

Sartre himself clearly states that his conclusion that the world is meaningless follows from his belief that God is dead. Just as Roquentin saw that rational humanism rests on the intrinsic value which men possess as created in the image of God, so Sartre sees that the entire edifice of values and beliefs about the meanings of things so carefully constructed by Western man is built solidly on the belief that God is *there*. With the foundation gone, Sartre logically concludes that the edifice cannot stand. Those aspects of human experience which have been seen as indicative of the overall scheme of things and man's place in it are merely what they are. They do not *mean* anything.

But all of this follows only from Sartre's belief

that God is dead, which is itself a metaphysical belief. We have noted that metaphysical beliefs of this sort can never be proved or established by scientific experiment or philosophical argument. They are themselves the embodiment of a fundamental stance toward existence.

Sartre has despaired. From the standpoint of his despair he perceives knowledge, experience, humanism (morality) and love as deceptions. From his perspective, they only cheat man by raising false hopes, hopes which cannot be cashed in.

I cannot prove, and perhaps no one can, that Sartre's decision to despair is the wrong decision or that his vision of a meaningless world is untrue. What I can show is the poverty of such a vision, that his vision does follow from a choice and that *this choice is not the only alternative open to twentieth-century man.* In the same world, with equal honesty, man may choose to hope.

Two Types of Despair

To understand hope we must distinguish between despair as a way of life and despair as a moment in life. Sartrean despair is despair as a way of life. And as a way of life, despair is essentially contradictory, for it is always the prelude to death.

The paradigm of despair is the moment when death is certain and final and there is no recourse. Despair as a way of life is living death. It is the knowledge that every action or decision I take is utterly futile. To live in despair is to be alive, but aware that my life is of no more consequence than a corpse. No experience, decision or accomplishment is of any significance; whether a deed is done or undone is infinitely trivial. Consistent despair leads to suicide, which is a serious problem for Camus and Sartre, one to which neither gives any ultimately satisfactory answer.

To hope is precisely to regard despair as only a *moment* in human existence. To be sure, if glib optimism is to be avoided and true honesty attained, despair is a *necessary* moment. It is that moment when a man faces suffering, misery and the reality of his own death and utters an anguished "Why?" It is the moment when he visualizes the awful possibility that the whole of existence may be a bad joke. In that moment it seems as if a man comes into being for no reason at all, lives for a few pointless years, always asking the absurd "Why?" only to vanish into the non-being from whence he came. This moment may recur again and again. But this despair is only a moment.

Clues toward Hope

The man who chooses to hope is rescued from the moment of despair by the call of life. He is alive and his life comes, as Thomas Howard has said, charged with evidences of meaning. The great poets, novelists and dramatists who have portrayed the saga of human existence in all its splendor and misery have been truthful. The call of life comes in a thousand wildly diverse forms: in moral experience, in personal relationships (friendship and erotic love), in the wonder of birth, in the ecstasy of music, in poetic communion with nature.

Consider morality, which we examined in the last chapter. The man who is firmly engaged in *living* is forced to acknowledge that some actions are right and others wrong. Hope takes this as a clue to what life is all about. It is not a matter of supreme indifference whether I shake a man's hand or break a man's neck. That what I do in life *matters* is as certain as my own death.

Consider love. When a man makes love to a woman, he chooses to uncover her beauty in private, not on a street corner. Why? Something magnificent, something mysterious lies in this ecstasy, which man marks and recognizes by pulling across it the veil of privacy. Try as he will man will never succeed in believing that this experience is a mere physical event, with no more *meaning* than shaking hands (which is also a physical event which has *meaning*).

Consider nature. In a simple evening walk in the woods or in the glories of a sunrise on the ocean, man encounters meaning. He cannot truly believe that it is unimportant that a river should flow or that the waves should dash against the shore. It strikes the man of hope that it is monstrous that the crisp smell of country air should be befouled by noxious fumes. From the snows of Kilimanjaro to the painted deserts of Arizona man has treasured nature, has acknowledged that the existence of these things matters. It is very difficult to agree with Camus' assessment of nature:

> At the heart of all beauty lies something inhuman, and those hills, the softness of the sky, the outlines of these trees at this very minute lose the illusory meaning with which we had clothed them, henceforth more remote than a lost paradise. [17]

Is the meaning found in nature illusory? The man who has been alone on a beach at sunset might truly argue that nothing could be more real than the beauty which he sees all around him.

What we are arguing is that the call of life is stronger than the call of death, that it is possible to *hope,* and see death for what it is, an alien intruder in a meaningful world. In every aspect of life, there are evidences, clues as it were, that point to meaning. They do not come complete with a comprehensive explanation; they do not say to man, "Here is a complete philosophy of what life is all about." But they do possess a "gut" validity, just as does morality, which is the most important of these evidences. They do say, "There is a point to life. These things matter; they mean something."

In the *moment* of despair, the honest man senses the fragility of this meaning. In the face of the absurdity of death, he questions the meaning of these things and demands to know why they are thus and why he is so. But the call of life is strong. In the continuing decision to live from one moment to the next, hope affirms that there is an overall framework, a reason why these things are significant.

Perhaps someone might object that this continuous decision to refrain from suicide is made not from hope, but from cowardice. Man does not value life; he merely fears death. However, even this fear of death is negative evidence of man's uncrushable belief in the value of life. For the nihilist, death represents nothingness. For him there awaits no God, no hell or heaven, only eternal silence. If a man truly believed in the rottenness of existence, if life were really nauseating, the cool solace of death would be welcome. In his very struggle against death, man affirms, even against his will, that there are meaningful distinctions, that at least one thing (life) is better than one other thing (death).

The moment of despair may be the trigger which, in motivating a man to question the meaning of his own existence, provides the prod to discern the meaning of his world. Hope is embodied in a concrete belief that, though there are mysteries and problems which man does not understand, there is a meaningful order to the universe, an order in which he has an important place.

Thus, as was the case with morality, to despair

of meaning may be precisely the trigger to an affirmation of the necessity and reality of meaning. An authentic hope which follows this affirmation must go on to discover just what areas of human life are significant, and what this significance points to. But one must decide to look. The existential moment of despair may stun a man, but it may also awaken him to what is significant in his world. If his eyes are opened, his gaze may be directed to those evidences and clues toward meaning which he must account for to truly understand himself and his world.

the
roots
of
despair
alienation

chapter 4

If hope is possible, why despair? The question is really double-edged. First, it may mean, "Why has twentieth-century man despaired?" If the evidences for hope and the call of life were so strong, how did post-Christian man lose his way? Or, second, the question may be interpreted on a more personal level. As each man looks at the world around him and into his own soul, why should he despair? If there are evidences, clues which point toward hope, shouldn't a man turn from the despair of night and face the day?

The Sickness unto Death

The second question is more important, but first

we must grapple with the former one: What is the condition of twentieth-century man? Where did he go wrong? When and how did hope become an illusion for him? Why has he turned to drugs, pornography, violence and mysticism?

It is obvious that the preliminary conclusion we reached in the preceding chapter (that it is self-evident that there are values) is inadequate to solve the human dilemma. Indeed, it is comically like the response of glib optimists who, confronted by the dismal wreck of civilized Western society, write letters to the editor to assure everyone that things are not really so bad and that the real problem is with the news media, which always seem to focus on the "bad" side of things. This attitude is epitomized in a popular song: "You'll see the sun come shining through, if you'll just *smile*."

In a somewhat analogous fashion, we have called out to a world in the throes of despair: "Just look at things the right way, and you'll see that the world really is meaningful." The problem of despair goes deeper than any such solution.

As Sören Kierkegaard wrote over a century ago, despair is the sickness unto death. To merely tell man that his world really is meaningful does not heal this sickness. Despair is precisely the sickness which robs the really meaningful of its meaning.

We have presented an intellectual argument that despair as a way of life is not man's only alternative. With equal or greater honesty he may choose to hope. But despair is not merely an intellectual problem. It is the sickness unto death, the disease which robs all human endeavors and relationships of their point. And a sick man requires more than arguments that his sickness is not necessary; he needs a remedy—a cure.

The point is that man is unable to hear the call of life because he is not truly living. His condition has been aptly labeled by novelists, sociologists, philosophers and theologians alike as *alienation*.

Hippies and Middle America

Man has always had a deep sensitivity for the harshness, cruelty and misfortune which accompany the good things in life. His greatest dramas have always been tragedies; no emotion is so universally shared or deeply felt as sorrow. Man has always recognized that there are forces in the universe which seem bent on destroying him, whether those forces be regarded as cosmic demons, blind natural laws or sociological structures.

Similarly, keen thinkers and moral reformers have always recognized that there is something at odds within man's own nature. Man's proclivity for actions which run counter to his own best interests is so marked that some psychologists have postulated the existence of a death wish lurking deep within the human psyche. Certainly the World Wars, Biafra, the situation in the Middle East and Viet Nam have made man's capacity for self-destruction abundantly clear, but man has always been very skilled in these matters.

This double-awareness that man is alienated or estranged to a certain degree from his universe, from his fellow man and from himself is not new, but it seems to have descended on modern man with particularly crushing force. Alienation is most visible in the strangely-garbed, long-haired youths who occupy certain sections of our nation's cities, throng to rock festivals and gather in small communes. Here I am not referring to youth in general, not to political revolutionaries and certainly not to every young person who has been labeled a "hippie." I am talking about people who in their own words no longer "care," who just don't see the point of trying. I am referring to teenagers for whom sex has already become jaded, who have "tried everything" and found it wanting.

Among these people, a distinctive life-style has arisen, centered on drugs, sex and music. Its proponents have, in their own words, "dropped out." Derided and ostracized by "normal" society, they are accused of having no "positive" alternative to offer. In some cases this charge is completely unjustified. However, even if the charge is true, sensitive thinkers of the subculture sometimes shrug off such an accusation as meaningless. Of course they have no "positive" solution. If they had a solution to offer, they would not pass their time staring idly on street corners or escaping into a fantasy drug world.

Not long ago I walked through the "Tight Squeeze" area of Atlanta, Georgia, which has become a mecca to the hippie subculture somewhat comparable to Haight-Ashbury a few years ago. As I looked at these once-hopeful flower children, I realized there are three possible attitudes one may adopt toward them.

Perhaps the most common attitude would be to bolster one's own ego by regarding them as "scum, long-hairs, weirdos, kooks," thereby placing oneself on a pedestal far above those who refuse to rest comfortably in the mold. It is always important to have some group or class to feel superior to, and as it is no longer quite fashionable to be a racist, hippies serve as invaluable scapegoats.

But there is a second way to view them, admittedly one adopted by only a small minority. One can glorify this community as a place where true love and concern is felt, a last refuge for human values. This attitude is occasionally taken by the news media which have gone on to paint a false and romanticized picture of the "gentle, flower-folk." But as I observed the situation, I instinctively felt that to picture this life-style as the beginning of utopia was as false and harmful as to adopt the attitude of the self-righteous.

The only emotion I could feel was compassion for human beings like myself who, confronted by the heartbreak of life, simply had no answer. I did not share their despair, but I could understand it. I could not judge them; neither could I glorify them. As I looked around me at faces which seemed sad and empty, I could only see these young men and women for what they were—children of the twentieth century. There, walking around—painted on the bewildered visage of a fourteen-year-old girl— was alienation, communicated far more vividly than I can depict in words.

It would be a tragic mistake to regard hippies as the only alienated segment of society. To do so would ignore the smouldering rage of suppressed minorities. But even more significantly it would ignore the unacknowledged and often unrecognized alienation which pervades all of society, including so-called Middle America.

The hippie community represents the small tip of a huge, submerged iceberg, an iceberg made up of the fears, miseries, anxieties and neuroses of "straight" society. Perhaps the hippie movement inspires such hostile reaction because it says openly what many dare not admit, even to themselves— that their lives are empty, devoid of human warmth and significant encounter.

Repetition characterizes Middle America. We watch the same television shows, drive the same cars, belong to the same clubs, perform the same repetitive tasks for roughly the same remuneration. Mass-production technology seems to conspire against our individuality; even our whims are molded by the insistent, ever-present TV commercial. When reaching for words to describe our culture, "plastic" and "sterile" increasingly come to mind. It is not surprising that the "call of life," as we have described it, is heard only with difficulty. We just don't know what it means to truly *live*.

Alienation in the Theater and Literature: Man of La Mancha and Catch-22

That modern man seems increasingly unable to face up to reality as he encounters it can be illustrated by a comparison of the musical *Man of La Mancha* with *Catch-22*, Joseph Heller's novel which has been put into theater form in a motion picture. Though these two may seem wildly diverse, the underlying attitude toward reality is strikingly similar.

Man of La Mancha is drawn somewhat freely from the life of Miguel de Cervantes and from Cervantes' immortal novel, *Don Quixote.* The musical opens with Cervantes being thrown into prison, awaiting the dreaded Spanish Inquisition. His fellow prisoners are a rough lot and do not take kindly to their new and literary comrade. In consequence they decide to put Cervantes on "trial" in their own kangaroo court fashion.

With his quick wit Cervantes thinks of a way to postpone the "court's" verdict, save his possessions and possibly even vindicate to them his own worth and the value of his calling. For his "defense" he will entertain the prisoners by telling and acting out a rousing good story. So begins the play within a play, the story of Don Quixote de la Mancha.

The story of Don Quixote, as told in *Man of La Mancha,* is not complicated. A simple country gentleman, getting on in years and down on his luck financially, imagines himself to be Don Quixote (not his real name of course), a glorious knight-errant such as supposedly roamed Europe several centuries earlier. The poor man has read so many tales of chivalry, full of knights of the round table and beauteous maidens and other such stuff, that he finally takes leave of his senses and imagines himself to be one of the characters he has read about.

Taking with him a somewhat dim-witted local farmer as his "squire," Don Quixote sallies forth to fulfill his knightly calling, which is of course to be a righter of wrongs and injustices, an enemy of evil-doers and a defender of beauteous maidens, honor and the code of chivalry in general. After an unfortunate joust with some windmills which the knight takes to be giants, Don Quixote spies a castle, which is in reality a tavern, where he thinks he might obtain a night's repose. At the tavern, among other things, Don Quixote takes a barber's shaving basin to be "the golden helmet of Mambrino," which as a glorious knight he simply must have. Such conduct as this soon convinces everyone that Don Quixote is quite mad.

Living at the "castle" is an ordinary tavern slut, Aldonza, who even refers to herself as a whore. In Don Quixote's eyes she is Dulcinea, his lady, the fairest of the fair and the purest of the pure. Aldonza is frankly puzzled by the treatment she gets from Don Quixote. The knight is respectful, kind, even worshipful. She seems disturbed yet touched by the knight's gentility.

Meanwhile, back on the home front things are none too good. Don Quixote's friends and relatives are concerned about his condition. Dr. Carrasco, Don Quixote's prospective son-in-law, is worried that the old man's pranks will give the family a bad name. Carrasco epitomized the shrewd, "this-worldly" person who has come to terms with reality. Not really evil, though perhaps not above cutting a few moral corners, he has nothing but contempt for starry-eyed, impractical idealists, and he feels an obligation to cure Don Quixote of his delusions.

For his therapy he confronts Don Quixote in the guise of another knight, the "Knight of Mirrors." He challenges Don Quixote to combat, to which he comes armed with mirrors. The mirror does not lie. When the old man sees himself as he really is, the truth will force him to come to terms with reality. And it does. The Knight of Mirrors (Carrasco of course) wins the joust, and Don Quixote returns home, an old, sick man.

But reality does not have the final word. Aldonza has been touched by Don Quixote's "madness." That someone else could actually see her as pure and noble, as someone who possesses *value,* changes her whole way of looking at herself. She feels she really is Dulcinea, and she must see her Don Quixote again. She goes to see him, gains entrance to the house and rejuvenates his spirits. Together, she and Don Quixote, even as he faces death, dare to "dream the impossible dream." Don Quixote dies, the unvanquished idealist, seeing the world as he wishes to see it, accepting it only on his own terms.

Cervantes' story is finished. The prisoners are impressed by the tale. It seems to give each of them, including Cervantes himself, fresh hope in their bleak situation. For Don Quixote, according to *Man of La Mancha,* represents Cervantes' own uncompromising attitude toward life. He is determined to live a life of hope, based on a world of justice, beauty and love, whether that world exists or not.

Man of La Mancha puts the issue plainly: The "insanity" of Don Quixote is to be preferred to the good sense and worldly wisdom of Dr. Carrasco. It is better to live in a make-believe world of chivalry and justice than to come to terms in a compromising fashion with the coarseness and injustice of "real" life. If this is escapism, it is at least a noble escapism. In the musical this is announced straightforwardly by the Padre who sings, "To each his Dulcinea," meaning that every man must have his own shining goal, no matter how illusory, "to keep him from despair." Every man must have something to live for; no matter that "she's only flame and air."

The novel *Don Quixote* itself is at least partly a satire on tales of chivalry, which were common at the time. *Man of La Mancha* captures those elements of *Don Quixote* which are particularly modern. To what extent is a man justified in building his life around values which perhaps are not part of the "real world" at all? Can a man construct a world for himself if the real world is unbearable? That such a problem should be felt so keenly clearly shows the depth of man's alienation from that "real" world. The ontological status of those qualities and values which make life livable has come into question.

Catch-22 is likewise a classic statement of the insanity of the "real" world. Both the movie and novel capture in a deep way man's current sense of alienation. In both art forms, the story is grim and funny, black comedy of a peculiarly modern sort.

The action centers around a U.S. Army Air Force base during World War II. The fictitious Mediterranean locale is Pianosa, from which an odd assortment of American flyers take off to deliver their bomb loads over northern Italy, and receive their share of flak, injuries and deaths.

Yossarian is a bombardier in this group, who with all his heart and soul wants one thing—to stay alive. Unfortunately, that task is complicated by his commanding officer, Colonel Cathcart. When the unit first arrived in Pianosa, twenty-five missions constituted a combat tour of duty. Upon fulfilling that task, a man was eligible to be relieved and rotated back to the States. However, just as some of the members of the wing, including Yossarian, had achieved or were nearing this figure, Colonel Cathcart arrived and celebrated his new command by raising the required number of missions from twenty-five to thirty. And he continued to raise the number of missions required—to thirty-five, fifty, even to sixty with no end in sight.

Trapped in a murderous situation, Yossarian looks for an out. Surely there must be a way; something must be done before he and his dwindling number of still living friends become nonentities. And of course there are "ways out." But each of them has a catch—Catch-22.

There is a rule that anyone who is insane must be grounded. Yossarian, whom everybody agrees is crazy as a loon, tries to take advantage of this rule. In one scene of the novel, he approaches the doctor and pleads to be grounded. The doctor informs him he is wasting his time, though he admits that there is a rule saying he has to ground anyone who is crazy. Yossarian tells him to ask any of the others and they will tell the doctor how crazy he is. The doctor meets this request with simple, insane logic. All the others are equally crazy; they have to be to keep flying murderous bombing missions. "And you can't let crazy people decide whether you're crazy or not, can you?"[1]

Of course this mere verbal jousting does not reveal the real power of Catch-22. Before anyone can be grounded for being crazy, he must *ask* to be grounded. But of course anyone with enough sense to ask to be grounded is not really crazy.

> There was only one catch and that was Catch-22, which specified that a concern for one's safety in the face of dangers that were real and immediate was the process of a rational mind. Orr [a friend of Yossarian's] was crazy and could be grounded. All he had to do was ask; and as soon as he did, he would no longer be crazy and would have to fly more missions. Orr would be crazy to fly more missions and sane if he didn't, but if he was sane he had to fly them. If he flew them he was crazy and didn't have to; but if he didn't he was sane and had to. Yossarian was moved very deeply by the absolute simplicity of this clause of Catch-22 and let out a respectful whistle.[2]

Catch-22 has other clauses and takes other forms, but the result is always the same; Yossarian is trapped. He is trapped in an insane world where men flying dangerous bombing missions would sell their parachutes and medical kits—and those of others—for money. His is a world in which planes vanish into clouds and men standing on beach rafts are sliced in two by airplane propellors. In such an insane world, insanity becomes sanity.

In the movie, Yossarian finally concludes that the sanest thing he can do is to jump in a small raft and attempt to paddle to neutral Sweden, a distance of only a few thousand miles! He escapes by following the modern counterpart to Don Quixote's world of make-believe; he embraces the absurd. If the world is insane, then isn't madness sanity? Yossarian, though crazy, is the sanest man in Pianosa.

Who in such a world would not feel alienated? These two very different products of modern art both aptly catch the concept and the feeling of modern man's alienation.

The Impact of Science and Technology

What are the causes of this alienation, this feeling of "homelessness?" One factor which many thinkers have pointed to is the pervasive triumph of Western science and the offspring of that triumph, the technological society. As scientific knowledge became the only respectable form of knowledge, man's picture of the world and himself changed tremendously. Religious faith began a steady and, so far, unreversed decline, particularly among the educated classes. The "ordinary" world full of colors, laughter, sounds, love, meaning and values was eroded and undermined by the scientific description of a "real" world, with only particles, masses, velocities and other such measurable quantities. The world was seen as a collection of brute unrelated facts. "Values," whatever they might be, were seen as man's own subjective creation. Even in the subjective realm "inside" man, however, "values" were not safe. Inevitably, man came to see *himself* as just another "fact" in a world of brute facts, something to be studied, explained and manipulated. The stage was set for *Brave New World.*

The roots of man's current estrangement were already seen in the nineteenth century. In *Notes from Underground* Dostoevsky showed his concern over the scientific and technological order which he clearly saw was becoming dominant in Western civilization. According to many social theorists of his day, the world was making steady progress toward a more just, if not perfect social order. The spearhead of this advance was science. The theory was that "man does nasty things only because he doesn't know where his true interests lie, that if he were enlightened about his true interest, he would immediately stop acting like a pig and become kind and noble."[3] Scientific knowledge, they said, will lead man out of the dark ages.

Dostoevsky replies that these theorists simply do not take into account man's free will and its perversity. The "scientist" replies quickly:

Ha-ha-ha! Strictly speaking there's no such

> thing as will! . . . Today, science has already
> succeeded in dissecting a man sufficiently to
> be able to tell that what we know as desire
> and free will are nothing but—[4]

Science will sooner or later discover *all* the real
causes of our whims and desires. When the laws
governing will have been discovered, then mathematical equations can be devised to make this a
better world. Science will ensure that men act in
their own best interests.

There is only one defect in this utopia, but
Dostoevsky feels that it is crucial. In such a world
men cease to exist. Real individuals disappear. All
that remain are organ stops or piano keys, "for
what is a man without will, wishes, and desires, if
not an organ stop?"[5]

The problem is simply this: Utopias are built by
reason for reasonable men, but there is more than
reason to man. And this "more" is very important;
it is what makes each man an *individual.* Although
reason and science are good, they must not be
allowed to encroach upon each man's individuality,
for it is more important than science, reason or any
possible scheme for the betterment of society.
And, in the final analysis, men know this, for

> . . . there is one instance when a man can wish
> upon himself, in full awareness, something
> harmful, stupid, and even completely idiotic.
> He will do it in order to *establish his right* to
> wish for the most idiotic things and not to be

obliged to have only sensible wishes.[6]

That this is so Dostoevsky considers to be good. To wish for something stupid and irrational may be the best thing a man can do.

Specifically it may be more advantageous to us than any other advantages, even when it most obviously harms us and goes against all the sensible conclusions of our reason about our interest—and because, whatever else, it leaves us our most important, most treasured possession: our *individuality*.[7]

The important thing is not to lose one's individuality. If science and rationality threaten to take that away, then I must repudiate science and rationality. Dostoevsky turns to the "absurd," the existentialist theme which recurs again and again.

It is not just abstract reason or theoretical science which has robbed man of his "humanness," but the practical outcome of that science—a technological society. Karl Jaspers, the German existentialist, gives a piercing analysis of this in his book, *Man in the Modern Age*. The technical life-order, through rationalization and mechanization, has now made possible the satisfaction of the elementary needs of an enormous population. Nevertheless, this technical life-order is precisely what threatens to annihilate the individuality Dostoevsky believed to be all-important.

In such a technical life-order, man is confronted by a world in which no objects are made by an individual just for his own purposes. Everything is mass-produced for mass consumption. Man's world becomes wholly made up of instruments to gratify immediate desires; such instruments are to be used and then discarded.

That this attitude toward objects has been transferred to other humans is only too evident when one reads the newspapers. And why not? Man does seem to be merely an object. The only point of his existence is to occupy a "function" in the overall technical order. That one man, John Appleby, exists is of no particular consequence. John Appleby has no meaning *qua* individual. He is not indispensable; because he is only a "function," he can easily be replaced by another. Man *is* an object—a cog in a vast machine.

Thus, science and technology have made a negative impact on man's view of himself and his world. But, as Jaspers notes, it would be foolish to blame man's alienation on science or technology alone—as if they were independent, external forces over which man has no control. Even if it were true that man today has no control over his creation, it was not always true. Science and technology are man's creation. Both had and have a great potential for both good and evil. Nuclear physics has produced both bombs and a treatment for cancer. If, therefore, they have been radically misused, then this misuse points to something radically wrong within man himself.

It is man who has chosen to value objects over people; it is man who has set up whatever establishment or apparatus controls his existence. To argue otherwise is only to degrade man further. If man's alienation is the inevitable result of inexorable historical, physical or natural laws, then man is further reduced in significance. He has become an object manipulated and determined by blind forces.

The Marxist View of Alienation

This is the error of Marx, at least as he is popularly understood, who was aware of man's alienation and sought to explain it in terms of economic and historical factors. Marx believed that all "values" are the product of human activity. The workers in the society of his day were completely divorced from the ownership of the means of production, and consequently from the power and material possessions which were rightfully theirs as the fruit of their labors. Noting this harsh exploitation of workers, Marx regarded the divorce of labor from the means of production as the cause of the workers' degradation to a mere animal-like existence of eating, sleeping, procreating and working. Thus man is not only alienated from material goods and possessions, but as a result of this, he is quite literally alienated from himself and from other men—hence, the class struggle.

This alienation was the inevitable result of the

historical forces Marx termed the dialectic (a term borrowed from Hegel). Marx thought historical change was the result of a clash of economic interests, with each stage of development noting a new system of economic production. Thus, capitalism had been preceded first by slavery and then by feudalism, each with a dominant class and an oppressed class. After the final overthrow of capitalism by the proletariat, these historical forces would, Marx believed, culminate in the overcoming of man's alienation in a classless society, a utopia of human equality and freedom. Marx believed that he had given a scientific demonstration of the truth of his thesis through an inductive study of history and economics.

In Marx we find the classic example of blaming man's alienation on the "system," or the "establishment." The source of man's alienation does not truly lie within a man but rather outside him. However, if such is the case, man's alienation is more far-reaching than Marx himself saw. He is alienated not only from himself but from the possibility of becoming himself. He is no longer free.

Of course, Marx would agree: Man is not free; he cannot be free until the utopia of the classless society is ushered in. But it is folly to pretend that Marx or anyone else has given or can give a scientific demonstration of the inevitability of any such future society. This is particularly true if history is, as Marx claimed, nothing but blind "matter in motion." If the Christian God is rejected, and along with God the notion of Providence, it is impossible to discern any necessary *telos* towards which history is moving. There is certainly little evidence of the classless society among those who consider themselves Marx's successors.

If a classless society is not inevitable, only positive action can bring it about, and of course Marx urged the proletariat to take that action. But if men are free to bring about utopia, they are also free *not* to bring about utopia. Men are free to exercise their greed, self-centeredness and prejudice—or perhaps to love. In short, a Marxist description of behavior, in which actions are controlled by economic forces, is a description of a state of alienation but not an adequate account of *why* man is alienated or how to overcome it.

No view which sees man as necessarily the slave of irrational forces can see him as truly human, because as Dostoevsky says, it robs man of his most treasured possession, his individuality. No man can truly *be,* can truly *act,* can truly *live* as a fully developed individual if he is not free—free to make mistakes, free to have "non-sensible" wishes, free to degrade his own freedom. Only on this condition is responsibility for one's actions—the first step toward a mature, humane existence—possible.

Alienation and Freedom

What does it mean to affirm that the alienation of

the individual is rooted in his own freedom? The answer of course depends upon the meaning given to the notion of freedom itself.

Man is the creature who reflects, but Aristotle misinterpreted the nature of this reflection when he *defined* man as a rational animal. Man does not merely think objectively, and abstract thinking does not capture the essence of self-consciousness. Man is a creature capable of stepping *outside* himself and reflecting on the meaning and worth of his own existence.

Man can distance himself from his own existence to a certain degree. He continually calls his own actions and himself into question. Thus, man is a *relation* of himself to his self. He has a self which he experiences as a "could be" or "ought to be," and he has a self which he experiences as an "actually is." Yet both of these together are his self.

This analysis of the nature of man is found in Kierkegaard's *The Sickness unto Death.* If we see man, with Kierkegaard, as a synthesis or a relation, the possibility of alienation is immediately obvious. Alienation will be seen as a misproportion in the relationship which constitutes the self. A gap opens between what a man would like to be or knows he ought to be and what he is. And yet man is unable to lose either half of the relation without ceasing to exist. He not only is what he is; he is also his awareness that he could indeed be something other than he is. If the separation of these two "selves" becomes too great, a man is torn apart.

Self-conscious freedom, though in itself a great boon, thus makes possible man's alienation. It is what distinguishes man from the beasts, and is the indispensable condition for man's efforts at self-improvement. The pathological condition results when this self-consciousness becomes self-hatred.

It is this self-hatred—the man who deep down has a real dislike for himself—that we wish to focus on. Certainly this fundamental self-contempt, often masquerading under the more innocuous title "inferiority complex," is widespread. And it is not pathological in the sense that it only characterizes a few "abnormal" people. Rather it is something which, to some degree, is experienced universally.

All pretension, all fronts, all masquerades, all attempts to present to the world a self which is other than one's real self are an indication that alienation is present. When a person feels he must hide behind a mask, create a "personage" which hides his real self, he reveals a shame over the self that he is. In fact, to the extent that a man hides his true self, he confesses that he does not truly value his self.

Furthermore, that men so desperately need acceptance from others is itself indicative of alienation. The man who continually has to make others aware of his own worth actually craves reassurance from the other that he is in fact worth something. We are all familiar with the man who in a discussion needs to make all the points, who in an argument needs to be always right, etc. Such a craving points to the man's inner belief that in fact he is not worth very much. Though not all of us exhibit such behavior, the tendency, I dare say, is recognizable in each of us.

Other evidences of a misproportion in the self are the frank statements of the man who admits, "If only I were so-and-so, I would be truly happy," or "If only I had a job which paid twice as much as this one, then...," or "If only I had a new vacation cottage in Florida, then...." These statements clearly express resentment over the fact that one has to be the self one is. The tragedy is, as Kierkegaard saw, that such a person does not even understand the source of his unhappiness; if his wish were granted, he would not really achieve the unification of himself he desires.

Perhaps the decisive expression of alienation lies in the phenomenon of guilt. In the anguish of remorse, one experiences the irreversibility of the past. Who has not in a heated moment said something which caused someone else pain and then five minutes later bitterly regretted the words? Though amends can be made, apologies said, etc., in a certain sense the act is done when done and cannot be reversed. Yet a man must live with his past as *his* past. To the extent that he is unable to face his past, a man is alienated from himself.

Man's alienation from other men and from nature can plausibly be described as a function of this estrangement from himself. The man who does not like himself cannot like his fellow man very much. He does not have the emotional strength to give; all of his life is a taking and grabbing—an attempt to make himself somebody at the expense of others. Then, too, if the alienation we have described is universal, this fact goes far toward explaining man's despoilment of nature. The man who has no self and thinks to acquire one through possessions, or through achieving power over something else, will naturally turn to nature (and his fellow man) as readily available, easily exploitable objects.

Guilt and Responsibility

A review of our argument is in order. This chapter is addressed, as is the whole of this book, not to "the public" nor to "philosophers" nor any other class or group, but to individuals *qua* human beings. I have here attempted to describe alienation from within, not to give an exhaustive sociological or psychological description. I first attempted to describe the mood of alienation so prevalent today, a mood with which few will have difficulty identifying. I then attempted to treat the historical roots of our current dilemma and explored the relationship of alienation to self-conscious freedom, stressing the universality of the phenomenon. I have not tried to "explain" alienation, but to make it clear that *no such explanation can be used with integrity to rationalize man's tendency to wallow in his own despair.*

We initially asked two questions. (1) Why *has* twentieth-century man despaired? (2) As each individual man looks within himself, why *should* he despair? If man is free (and each of us persists in believing that he is), then the historical or scientific explanation which will serve as an answer to question (1) cannot be adequate as an answer to question (2).

To say that man has despaired because he has become strikingly conscious of his alienation from himself, other men and nature is only too true. To say that an individual is in despair because he is experiencing that alienation may also be true. For the individual to realize this truth may be important. But it is not enough.

The individual must also ask the question, "*Why am I in this state of estrangement?*" in an existential sense, and he must look for the answer within himself. If he does not do so, he cannot know whether it lies within his power to overcome his alienation. Before he can truly come to grips with his alienated mode of existence, he must acknowledge how deeply his estrangement is rooted in his own freedom. He must acknowledge that his unhappiness with himself and his inability to happily coexist with his fellow humans and nature, and his resulting feelings of guilt stem from his own pride and greed, from his fundamentally self-centered way of life.

It may be that when a man has undergone this self-analysis, he will conclude that he is powerless to overcome the gap between what he is and what he knows he ought to be. But if this should turn out to be the case, it still does not mean that man is not responsible for his condition. As Aristotle once said, to say that a man is free to throw a stone or not to throw a stone does not mean he is free to recall the stone once it has been thrown. Similarly, to say that a man is powerless to become the man he ought to be does not mean he is not responsible for being the man he has become. Rather, if this is man's condition, it then becomes his responsibility to look for help outside himself.

Passing through the Moment of Despair

If a man has become an alcoholic, he may well be a slave to his "habit." Literally incapable of refusing a drink, he is no longer free in any real sense. This of course does not mean that he was never free and therefore not responsible for his own condition. Somewhere along the line, there was a "first time" and many other times when he could have refused, particularly if he was aware of the dangers of excessive drinking. If society is compassionate (which is unfortunately not always the case), it will recognize that the alcoholic is a sick person, that he is incapable of healing himself apart from outside help. And society can do this without denying the man's personal responsibility for his condition.

How then can the alcoholic be cured? Certainly not by wallowing in self-pity and blaming his drinking habit on his wife, his mother or father, his job or society in general. Nor will he be cured if he attempts to hide his problem from himself and others. He can engage in little charades, drink when no one else is around, tell himself he just has "a few too many occasionally," but if he really is an alcoholic, his problems will only be aggravated by his concealment and self-deception.

To be cured, he must face up to his condition and to his own responsibility for it, and he must desire with all his soul to be healed. If he truly does this, he can perhaps turn to Alcoholics Anonymous or to some hospital or program of therapy. But if he will not even acknowledge he has a problem, and if he does not truly want to be helped, all such efforts will be useless.

We have been discussing a different type of sickness, the sickness unto death. The sickness of despair is rooted in and clearly tied to man's alienation from himself and his world. No man can overcome this sickness without acknowledging his own responsibility for it (and the accompanying responsibility to change it) and striving with all his being to overcome his alienation.

Imagine a situation where two men are engaging

in some cruel action, say severely beating a helpless dog. Assume that one of these men is so warped in his attitudes and values that he feels no guilt, while the other man, who began the beating in an emotional frenzy, soon becomes aware of the sickening character of the deed and is overcome with revulsion at himself. It is clear that the first man, the man who feels no guilt and is not even aware that he is doing anything wrong, is more evil than the second man.

Some might argue that the "average man" (any man who outwardly seems content in life) is not "alienated" or "in despair." Indeed, he might say that the "average man" would hardly know what the words mean. If this is true, then it would by no means follow that such a person would not be in despair. Indeed, it would follow that his despair goes deeper than the despair of the man who knows he is in despair, because he is one step further from the possibility of overcoming that despair and achieving the unification of his self. Despair is not primarily a psychological attitude; it is a way of life based on nothingness, or upon something which turns out in the end to be nothing.

Here, then, is why we have explored the depths of despair, and distinguished between despair as a moment and despair as a way of life. In earlier chapters we saw how the moment of despair may stun a man, may open his eyes to those aspects of his experience which point toward hope. We now see that given man's general condition of alienation, the *moment* of despair is essential if one is to overcome a life of despair. Before man can truly find himself at home in the world and with himself, he must honestly acknowledge his plight and his responsibility for it, and he must authentically strive to overcome his condition.

the overcoming of **despair** hope

chapter 5

How can man's alienation be overcome? We have seen that this abstract question must be replaced by an intensely personal one: How can I overcome my alienation?

Man the Traveler

Alienation is always a separation—a split, a tearing, an estrangement. The man who feels the need to regard his own life as ultimately significant and yet firmly believes that his "self" is no more than a chance configuration of atoms is literally torn apart. The man who recognizes his unconditional obligation to love his neighbor but who also knows in his heart that his whole life is oriented toward the satisfaction of his own desires likewise lacks wholeness. The man who feels that life is only worth living in community and that only a genuine I-Thou relationship could make life worthwhile and yet feels dreadfully alone and cut off from every genuine human contact is truly estranged from himself. The man who earnestly desires to feel a sense of oneness with nature but is stifled by his knowledge that he is only "projecting" personal qualities onto a brute, indifferent universe is caught in the grip of alienation. All these splits or rifts in a man surely lead to despair—a life in which a man is unable to affirm that living has any meaning or point.

Yet even this despair may be, as we have constantly affirmed, the prelude to its own transcendence, a prelude to hope. The individuals we have just described are surely closer to wholeness than the man who does not even feel the need to regard his own life as ultimately significant, or the man who pursues his own gratification without a thought for his neighbor. The man who desires an I-Thou encounter is surely closer to closing the gap between himself and his fellow man than the man who feels he needs no one but himself. Similarly, the man who desires to feel a reverence for nature is closer to finding the continuity he seeks than is the man who crassly sees the world as merely an object to be manipulated.

In a very profound sense, when a man recognizes

his responsibility for who he is and what he has become, and when he sees his obligation to become the person he ought to become, then meaninglessness has already been overcome. For as Viktor Frankl notes in *Man's Search for Meaning,* the answer to the abstract question "What is the meaning of life?" is in a sense already given when a man recognizes that *he* is the one being asked. Existence itself confronts every man and asks, "What meaning have you discovered and appropriated in *your* life?" Man is far along the road to a truly meaningful, spiritual existence when he recognizes that he is no idle spectator of the course of history, but is under an unconditional obligation to give his life significance.

Perhaps it is going too far to say that the meaning of life *is* a constant search for meaning. A search must have an object (or at least the hope of finding an object) to be meaningful. But it is not extreme to say that the recognition that life is a search is the *foundation* for a meaningful life.

Gabriel Marcel has defined man not as *homo sapiens* but as *homo viator* (man the traveler). The human condition is aptly characterized as a journey, a pilgrimage; man is a traveler, searching as Abraham did for a city "which hath foundations." The search is a continuing one; no man concludes it with finality in this life. No man can say, "There, I have done enough." No man can say with utter certainty, "Here is the final answer for all of life's problems."

We thus face life not as neutral observers, but as participants in a struggle which involves tremendous risk. The risk could be no greater; at stake is the existence of my *self*. I cannot face the problem of my alienation with the objectivity of a scientist or mathematician. No computer can produce the answers I require. There are no coercive arguments or logical machinery which can crank out a "final solution."

This is not to say I am excused from intellectual honesty. Certainly I must seek real answers to real questions. It is only apathy that is forbidden. I cannot merely sit back in my evening chair and idly speculate on whether the world is in fact meaningless and despair is therefore justified. If the world is truly meaningless, it is cause for weeping and gnashing of teeth, not polite reflection. Nevertheless, my own steadfast consciousness of my own obligation to live significantly belies this nightmare world.

I hear a call—a still, clear call. Perhaps the call is an illusion, but still I hear the call. And I must answer.

The Barrier to Becoming Whole

To answer the call I must choose. What must I choose? I must choose *myself*. I must choose a way of life, a ground and measure for my existence, a focal point for all of the finite decisions I must make.

Such a choice may be and perhaps usually is unconscious. It is exhibited and tested only in the concrete existence of an individual.

But the problem is precisely that I am unable to choose myself. I am alienated from myself and cannot be the man I want to be. We must not ignore or slight the depth of man's alienation. That a man's alienation is rooted in his own freedom, that he recognizes his own responsibility for his condition, does not mean that he will be strong enough to overcome that alienation. Man's condition is described by St. Paul in a famous passage.

> I do not even acknowledge my own actions as mine, for what I do is not what I want to do, but what I detest. But if what I do is against my will, it means that I agree with the law and hold it to be admirable. But as things are, it is no longer I who perform the action, but sin that lodges in me. For I know that nothing good lodges in me—in my unspiritual nature, I mean—for though the will to do good is there, the deed is not. The good which I want to do, I fail to do; but what I do is the wrong which is against my will; and if what I do is against my will, clearly it is no longer I who am the agent, but sin that has its lodging in me. (Romans 7:15-20, NEB)

Here Paul captures man's plight in terms of a war or struggle between two natures. He realizes that when a man does not do what in his innermost being he truly wants to do, then he is not man in the fullest sense. It is not his self which controls his actions, but something alien to man's true self. Hence, despair results. Paul is saying, "Don't you know where your anguish and despair come from? That terrible condition of being separated from one's self, of hating one's own actions, is caused by sin. Your failure is moral."

It would perhaps be merciful on my part not to strengthen this point by quoting my evening newspaper and illustrating man's moral failures. There really is no need for lurid descriptions of My Lai and Biafra to an age which has seen a war presented nightly on the six o'clock news, complete with body counts. There is no need to describe even the less violent and subtle ways man has found to make his existence a tortured one.

Kierkegaard says in *Fear and Trembling* that an ethic which disregards sin is a perfectly idle science. Similarly, any program of action, description of the good life or utopian social plan which disregards the facts of human nature is merely a thought-exercise, however noble or beautiful an exercise it may be. So the question remains: *How* can I choose myself?

A Thought Experiment

While we are on the subject of thought-exercises, let us perform one ourselves. Let us temporarily

suppose an old and venerable, but somewhat un-
stylish belief to be true.

Let us suppose that there is a God. Let us suppose that the millions of prayers addressed to him
through the ages have been heard. Let us suppose
that God's nature is love, and that he is a being
more like a person than anything else in human
experience, that he lacks only specifically human
foibles and imperfections and far surpasses man in
every perfection. Let us suppose that the world
was created by God and continues to exist each
instant by virtue of God's power. Finally, let us
suppose that man occupies a very special place in
that creation. Indeed, let us suppose that man was
created in the image of God (*imago Dei*), with a
potentiality for either communion with the God
who is both ground and measure of his being or for
prideful revolt against his Maker and a constant
striving for autonomy. Quite a lot to suppose,
really, but perhaps the trick can be carried out
with some imagination.

Now of course we are only supposing, but on
such a supposition man's condition might be con-
strued to be something like the vision of man
found in twentieth-century existentialist literature.
That is, having chosen the option of prideful revolt, man's condition is that of alienation from his
true self. Let us elaborate on this description as
one might who believed this supposition to be true.

God gave man a nature—an end or purpose for

living, if you will. That end or purpose was to exhibit in God's creation the nature of God himself and to live in perfect communion with God. To exhibit God's nature is to exercise in finite terms appropriate to man those aspects of God which are evident to man—his goodness, love and creativity.

But man, as befitting a creature made in God's image, was given the freedom to choose himself. In his pride man refused to choose the self offered him by God. He refused to relate himself to his Creator in love and desired to establish his own being. In short, every man desired what was right in his own eyes.

Still, God's image remains. Man feels the call of goodness, creativity and love; he realizes he is not truly *man* apart from these, but merely a calculating animal. In traditional terms, man has fallen and is painfully aware that he has fallen. He is alienated, conscious of guilt, prone to despair.

Supposing this all to be the case, what action would a loving God take? It seems clear that a God who truly loved his creation would not descend in wrath and destroy mankind, saying in effect, "The whole business was a mistake. I shall either have to start all over again or else forget the whole enterprise."

Rather, a truly loving God would be passionately concerned with the redemption of his creation, with the restoration of man to his intended place and role. Yet how could this be accomplished without robbing man of the freedom which gives him the potentiality for God-likeness? It could only be done by God encountering man in love and hoping man would respond—in love.

Continuing our thought-experiment, we can detect two problems connected with this idea. The first problem is twofold. It concerns man's actual fallen condition. Could God simply "forget" or "wink at" all the terrible crimes man has perpetrated? Though at first thought it might seem to be the loving thing to do, such action on God's part would amount to a repudiation of his own character. Could God, who is altogether righteous and just, condone man's unrighteousness and injustice?

The second aspect of this first problem concerns man's inability even to respond to God's love. It may be that man has become so mired in his own desire to have things his own way that he is literally incapable of "reforming" himself. That is, something within himself, perhaps shame, guilt, fear or his own perversity and pride, might prevent man from responding to God in love.

But there is still a second problem in the idea of God encountering man—the metaphysical problem of the incommensurability of the infinite and the finite. This problem is expressed in the Old Testament belief that a man could not look upon God's face and live. How could an infinite God encounter finite man without "overpowering" him? How could man retain the freedom to respond or not to respond?

This problem is analogous to the problem of the splendid and mighty king who loved a simple, peasant maiden.* If the king wooed her as the king, dressed in splendid robes and accompanied by courtiers and servants, could he ever really be assured of the girl's love? Could he be sure that the girl truly loved him, and was not merely awed or frightened by his power, or desirous of his wealth and the benefits of being queen? Of course in the fairy tale the king woos the maiden by adopting a disguise, by courting her incognito.

Now we are not telling a fairy tale, but performing a thought-experiment. Yet there seems to be something in the notion of God encountering man incognito. Perhaps—but the thought is almost unthinkable—God could encounter man as man.

Could God become a man? Could God become an existing, finite individual, bound up with all the frailty, desires and weaknesses of the human condition? The idea is too much; it is a paradox, the most paradoxical of paradoxes.

For there is an important difference between the fairy tale and our thought-experiment. In the fairy tale, the king assumed a disguise for a time, but he did not really give up his throne, while we have planted the audacious thought that God could become a man—finally and irrevocably. That a king

*The example is taken from Kierkegaard's *Philosophical Fragments.*

or emperor could give up his throne and be content to live out his days as a gardener or servant—that is difficult to conceive. But that God could become man—that is more than difficult; it is impossible.

Perhaps. From the viewpoint of finite wisdom, which craftily advises a man never to give of himself without seeing "what's in it for him," it is impossible to understand. But if there were a God, and we are only saying "if," it is eminently possible. For, by becoming man, God could effectively deal with the *first* problem posed, that of man's fallen condition.

By becoming man, God could effectively demonstrate that it is possible to live without compromising or going back on one's true self. By becoming man, God could give to man profound teaching, deepening and widening man's faulty and fragmentary conception of what a truly good life would be by giving man direct knowledge of God's nature. But most important, by becoming man, God could deal effectively with human *guilt*.

Let us now suppose that God truly did become man, that he not only had a body, ate food, etc., but that he truly took on himself the human condition. We now have God, altogether righteous, everything a man could be or hope to be, taking on himself man's actual condition. To conquer alienation and despair, God takes them upon himself—and overcomes them! In taking them upon himself, God takes on himself the pain and guilt which result from man's sin.

Considered religiously, and of course this is a religious thought-experiment, man's alienation and despair *are* the result of sin, man's willful repudiation of his own nature and God. God himself must close this gap, if it is to be closed at all. By overcoming and destroying man's guilt in his own case as man, God would in effect be promising every man that his personal guilt—and its harmful effects—could also be destroyed by God's righteousness.

If to overcome the problem of sin, God were to take such action, which could only arise out of infinite, incredible love, the twofold problem of guilt would be met. God, without negating his own character, could accept man, even though man remains fallen. God himself, who is perfectly righteous and just, would have suffered man's suffering and overcome it. He could then accept unrighteous and unjust man, because in a real sense God would have taken away man's guilt by placing it upon himself. And then, by overcoming that guilt, in a real sense destroying it.

If man were to respond to God in love, some action was needed on God's part to give man the ability to respond while allowing him the freedom not to respond. God's act of taking away man's guilt would be precisely what is required. Man could then respond by accepting God's acceptance, by believing God has truly acted to remove his guilt. If a man knew that God had accepted him *as he is,* on the basis of God's own promise that man is to become what he ought to be, he would have the courage to accept himself concretely, while choosing the self he is to become. Freed from the treadmill of guilt, self-hate and self-pity, man would be secure, accepted as he is. But accepted, not to stagnate, but to act. He is freed to choose his true self, a choice which is a daily striving, a constant renewal, a continual, concrete actualization.

What would that choice involve? Nothing else but the realization of man's original purpose: the exhibiting of God's character through a right relation to God himself and his creation. Such a choice would be a choice of love, justice and creativity as man's chief ends. It would exclude self-righteousness, for whatever a man is he would owe to God. Since God is personal, it would require the recognition of personality as the ultimate good of the universe, excluding the treatment of any human being as a foil for selfish gratification. It would require a recognition that I *am* my brother's keeper, and that every man is my brother.

It would also exclude the arrogance which characterizes man's present relationship to nature and require the humility to recognize the beauty in nature as a *gift* to be reverenced and enjoyed. To be sure, it would be a gift given for intelligent use, not to be wantonly destroyed or abused for unnecessary and frivolous amusements and comforts, or as is too often the case, positively immoral ends.

An Existential Testimony

By now the reader is probably quite bored by all this pretension. Justifiably, one might complain, "What a silly, pompous fool this fellow is, spinning out this long charade of a thought-experiment. Why does he play games with us and pretend to be doing thought-exercises, when everyone knows he has merely presented us with ordinary Christianity, which, if it is a hypothesis, is in any case neither new nor his own invention, being almost 2,000 years old."

Quite so, astute reader! I am overjoyed that you recognize Christianity for what it is, and not for what millions of supposed Christians take it to be. Far from pretending to make the whole business up, I willingly acknowledge that the scheme is far too fantastic for my limited ingenuity. Even the idea of presenting Christianity in this way is not original with me, but belongs to another.*

The point is, if this is indeed Christianity, then a man cannot be neutral towards it. For it represents an attempt to answer the problem of man's despair and alienation. Perhaps it's the true answer, perhaps not. But *if true,* it is an answer. The honest, existing individual who recognizes both his own

*Consult Kierkegaard's *Philosophical Fragments.*

alienation and tendency to despair but who desires with all his heart to give his life significance and purpose cannot remain indifferent toward this possibility.

If a man chooses to believe in Jesus Christ, that is his own decision. No parent, minister, theologian or philosopher can make such a choice for him. Least of all could *I* make such a choice for anyone. No rational arguments can remove the objective uncertainty and doubt which may attack a man in the stillness of the night, alone with his thoughts. To the existing individual who wishes to be faithful to himself, however, one path is closed: the path of the agnostic—the man who concludes that the "evidence" is not great enough on either side and hence simply lives out his life *ignoring* the question of the truth of Christianity or of any other comprehensive answer to life's problems.

I have chosen to believe that Jesus Christ is God. Preposterous? Perhaps. Paradoxical? To the highest degree. But nevertheless I believe.

When I read the New Testament I read a familiar story. Yet approached with the passion which befits it, the story becomes a burning and gripping tale, regardless of whether I'm reading it for the first, second or thousandth time.

In that story, I encounter Jesus Christ, a man who claims to be God. In his life, death and resurrection, I see my thought-experiment as an historical account, fleshed out with concrete detail, and hence even more wonderful than it seemed as fantasy.

Jesus' life: God becoming man and demonstrating to man that a life based on love is possible. I see Jesus healing the sick, feeding the hungry, giving hope to the downtrodden, teaching man to *love* even his enemy.

Jesus' death: God becoming alienated and taking on himself the ultimate result of human alienation and despair. I see Jesus, as a man, *separated from God,* crying out in agony, "My God, my God, why hast thou forsaken me?"

Jesus' resurrection: God as man, overcoming man's alienation and despair, becoming whole again, and in that wholeness offering *life* to every man, declaring that death is not the final word. I see Jesus destroying alienation and despair and opening to each existing individual the possibility of removing his own alienation and despair.

This Jesus whom I encounter speaks the truth, and, even more than that, he *is* the truth. On the basis of his testimony and his life, I believe that God has accepted me as I am, that I have been given the task of becoming what I ought to be and that God will ultimately recreate me so as to be precisely that—a creature reflecting his image.

The Path Traversed: A Road to Hope?

We began by seeking an answer to the question of whether man can overcome despair and attain hope. The question initially was, "Is hope possible?" In certain areas of human experience, even in the midst of despair, we uncovered existential evidence that hope was indeed a living possibility for man. In morality, personal encounter and esthetic experience we found hard cores of meaning, which should enable man to affirm that life is meaningful.

We were then forced to backtrack to the question, "If hope is possible, why is man in despair?" Why does the world appear meaningless to so many sensitive thinkers? The answer to this question lay in that pervading phenomenon we described as alienation. Man is unable to seize on those aspects of his existence which point to hope because of his estrangement from himself, other men and nature, and because of the resulting guilt.

Thus the question, "Is hope possible?" ultimately became, "How can I overcome my alienation?" This is an existential question which only a concretely existing individual can answer. We were, however, able to see that the two necessary conditions for an answer were (1) that a man assume the responsibility for his own condition and (2) that he acknowledge his unconditional obligation to change his condition.

Thus, the abstract question which despairing man asks, namely, "What meaning does life have?" is replaced by the question which is asked *of* authentic man (the man who acknowledges his guilt and responsibility), namely, "How can I give my life meaning and significance?" With this question we have moved from the realm of supposed neutrality and the constant arguments which convince only the convinced to the realm of a community of men engaged in a common search.

In this community no one dares to announce that the search is useless or that it has no object. Here there is no relief that, with such serious stuff removed, man is free to "forget" by immersing himself in immediacy. No, each member of the community, when alone with himself, may admit that it is possible that the search is futile, but he will not and cannot admit that this nightmare is really the case until the search is *completed*.

And, of course, this is impossible. The search cannot be completed in an ultimate sense in this life. One cannot "prove" the search is pointless any more than one can "prove" that he has found the definitive answer.

This is the community of those who recognize that they are called upon to *choose*. Each man chooses for himself, with complete responsibility for the choice. With this affirmation that hope is possible through a *choice* of a very distinctive nature, we arrive at the threshold of hope. The road through despair has been long and arduous. At the threshold another question looms, perhaps the most important yet posed. *Why* should a man choose one option over another? Why have I chosen Christianity? How can a man make such a choice? He must make the decision, but are there any guides to point the way, any criteria which his choice should meet?

Making the Choice

Man must choose himself and, in choosing himself, choose a framework for existence in which he has a place. By this decision he chooses a "way of life."

What we are interested in now is *how* a searcher makes such a choice. Note that the question of *how* does not arise outside the community of searchers. Only those who say, "Yes," to the question of *whether* one ought to give his life meaning can be concerned with *how* to make the choice.

Perhaps the reader is now sure that I am playing games with him. Did I not announce only a few pages back that I had made such a choice, and, indeed, did I not spell out the content of that choice (namely Christianity) in some detail? And did I not further argue that every such choice was fundamentally incapable of being "proved" and that it was a personal decision for which each man is alone responsible? Why then this question, "How can I make such a choice?"

All this I willingly admit and reaffirm. The question, "How can I choose?" when asked in the sense I mean to ask it, really amounts to, "How can this choice be justified?" From an external viewpoint, this question does *not* arise. That is, within the community or outside it, no interrogator has the right to demand of a chooser that he justify his choice to the interrogator. No man should arrogantly seek to destroy another's choice by demanding a proof which will convince *him*.

However, the question, "How can I make this choice?" when asked in another sense, can and ought to arise for the searcher. We can still imagine one member of the community approaching another and asking him how he justified his choice. When asked in the spirit of the community, the question means, "Could you, as a fellow searcher, shed some light on my decision? Why did you choose this way rather than the other?" When asked in this sense, it is really not an external question at all, because the questioner wants to know, "How did *you* justify this choice to *yourself*?"

This is the question we mean to uncover. It is the question which requires no external interrogator. Every true member of the community who chooses asks it of himself. "*Why* did I choose this way?" "In choosing this way, what guides am I relying upon?"

From this perspective, I see that though I am not responsible for producing a proof that will satisfy another, I am responsible for finding reasons which satisfy myself. And it is even possible that I will turn out to be the harsher critic of the two. It is *my* being which is at stake.

Otherwise the matter becomes infinitely easy. How can I give my life meaning? Easy. Choose a framework and way of life which will enable me to see my life as meaningful. Believe anything which satisfies my own needs.

How can such a choice be made? Here is the difficulty. When this question is understood rightly, the matter of choosing will not be "easy." One does not merely lash around for a likely possibility, then choose to believe that this is how things are. The question must continually be asked, "*Is* this how things are?"

The point is identical with one made earlier concerning intellectual neutrality and honesty. On such a question as "How can I give my life meaning?" a man cannot be neutral. To be neutral merely means not to recognize the question as legitimate. But honesty is not excluded: It is required. If a man does not answer the question honestly, he too has not recognized the question as legitimate.

Viktor Frankl, the famous Viennese psychiatrist, summed up the whole matter in his discussion of the will to meaning in *Man's Search for Meaning.* Man is driven by a will to meaning, such that he is forced to recognize his obligation to give his life meaning. Yet a man must not believe the meaning which he has given his life is merely illusory, or that he has merely invented a framework or set of beliefs which do not correspond with how things really are.

If the meaning that is waiting to be fulfilled

by man were really nothing but a mere expression of self, or no more than a projection of his wishful thinking, it would immediately lose its demanding and challenging character; it could no longer call man forth or summon him.[1]

There is of course a type of psychological reductionism which makes all of a man's important beliefs illusory by interpreting them as the result of unconscious forces. With this view we are not concerned. For, if all important beliefs are the result of unconscious forces, then this form of psychological reductionism is itself the result of some unconscious force. It too would be a form of wish fulfillment, the wish being the desire for the perverse satisfaction of destroying others' beliefs.

Rather than reducing religious beliefs to the result of unconscious psychological forces, we can more plausibly regard such a psychological reductionism as itself the result of a religious "choice" in the sense in which we have described choice. Here, however, the choice is a choice not to choose, the theory being the justification of that choice. Frankl again states this point clearly:

As soon as we have interpreted religion as being merely a product of psychodynamics in the sense of unconscious motivating forces, we have missed the point and lost sight of the authentic phenomenon. Through such a misconception, the psychology *of* religion often becomes psychology *as* religion, in that psychology is worshipped and made an explanation for everything.[2]

It is therefore necessary and legitimate for me to justify my choice; that is, to honestly ask myself what my reasons are for believing Christ to be God and whether those reasons are good ones. In doing so, it is as if I allowed someone else to overhear me by accident. The intent is not to make anyone else's choice for him, or remove from anyone else the "fear and trembling" which must accompany such a choice.

It is important to realize that an existential choice as we have described it is not something which is made once for all time. The task is never complete, hence neither is the choice. One must continually rechoose one's self.

For this reason, the justification of the choice is likewise never complete. At any moment, it is appropriate for a man to put his choice in question.

Hope through Faith

Why have I chosen to believe that Jesus Christ is God? There are three criteria which I believe any supposed answer must satisfy to be regarded as true.

First, the answer must at least be a satisfactory candidate, one which answers man's fundamental need. That is, it must be an answer which enables me to choose myself. The problem is not just that of finding an answer; an essential aspect of the problem is my own inability to choose myself because of my alienation and accompanying cycle of guilt and recrimination. Of course, just because an answer assuages psychological guilt feelings does not ensure that it is true. But at least it makes it a candidate to be considered.

And if a man realizes that his problem is not merely that of assuaging guilt-feelings but that of finding forgiveness for actual guilt, then it must be a characteristic of any purported answer that it offer to him forgiveness. And of course the man who assumes the responsibility for his own alienation realizes precisely this.

The whole point of the thought-experiment was to show that Christianity purports to offer man exactly what he needs—forgiveness. God accepts a man *as he is,* and thus enables him to choose himself concretely, replete with flaws and warts. And with this forgiveness as a base, a man can begin to choose his true self; he can become open to the power of God which remakes an individual in God's own image.

Secondly, to believe that an answer is a true answer I must believe that it corresponds to the way things are. That is, any framework (a view of myself and my relationship to other men and nature) which gives my life meaning, must be a framework which makes sense of my experience. Apart from experience, I have no way of knowing how things are; hence the test of a framework will be its power to satisfy all aspects of my experience, particularly those areas which I regard as most valuable and important.

It is here that we must return to chapters two and three and the areas of experience described there. Even in despair, my experience—of the necessity of morality, of the meaningfulness of encountering another person in love and of being caught up in the beauty of human creations and of nature—possesses a "gut" validity. Whatever else a framework must incorporate, it must make sense of these "signals of transcendence."

These areas of experience seem best understood to me when interpreted in the light of an actually existing personal God. From this perspective, the basis of morality can be seen in the value of *personality*. God, as the Supreme Person, possesses infinite value and, as the creator of all other persons, has endowed them all with value. The moral "ought" can then be interpreted as God's command to acknowledge *his* ultimate value and, in doing so, acknowledge the value of *every* person. In the words of Kant, "Treat every man as an end, and never as a means only." This is of course implied by Jesus' formulation of the essence of morality, "Thou shalt love thy neighbor as thyself."

The one who believes in God can also make sense of love. He can regard the experience of love, not as a mere transitory feeling, but as the most important aspect of human experience, the chief "clue" as to the meaning and significance of being a man. Man is someone worth loving; he is in fact loved by a supremely worthy being. The true meaning of being a person is to love—and to be loved.

That nature is beautiful, that she is orderly, that she can at times even seem divine is likewise not a mystery, if she is viewed as a divine creation. Man's attitude towards nature has always been ambivalent. At times, nature appears to be destructive, terrifying, amoral—at other times, beautiful, awesome, the most meaningful aspect of existence. The question is, "Which is nature's true face?"

A pure naturalism can see nature only as blind, amoral, at best "neutral." The meaning we import to her must be seen as illusory. But, if there is a God, then there lurks behind nature's beauty not merely brute force, but personality. It is therefore natural for man to feel kinship with nature. The other side of nature, what is termed "natural evil," is rightly viewed as an aberration, another mark that the world is not what it was meant to be.

That man is capable of creating a Beethoven symphony and a Sistine Chapel ceiling also seems more compatible with a view that sees man as made in the image of the one who created the heavens and the earth. When truly appreciated, a work of art is incapable of complete rational explanation; it arouses awe and wonder that transcends reason. If an eternal God exists, there is a basis for the overwhelming feeling one has when experiencing a work of art, the feeling that he is in the presence of something immortal.

Ultimately, it is the existence of man himself that I am appealing to. Honest man sees that there is something about himself which transcends the pseudo-scientific category of the perfectly natural. Man's very need for meaning is part of that something. What gave rise to a creature with such deep-felt *spiritual* needs? I can best understand myself as a creature made in God's image, created to commune with God.

That God became man may seem highly improbable. However, the very first sentence of the thought-experiment, the first "if" of the hypothesis, represents the crucial step—"If God exists. . . ." If God's reality be granted, the rest follows, not by logical necessity, but at least with a logic of plausibility. Thus, if there is indeed a God, it is at least possible that the man Jesus was in fact God, as he claimed to be. The challenge is then to explore the New Testament, to see if Jesus' words and deeds ring true.

The third characteristic which a true answer must have is that it must be able to be *lived*. It cannot merely be a theory spun out in the study or the church and forgotten in the world of action. A man must be able to carry it with him every minute of every day. If it does not work in his life, it is no answer.

Thus, an answer must actually enable a man to begin to overcome his alienation in existence, not completely, but in a constant striving. It must enable a man to begin to act morally, to love, to create; in short, to begin to be himself truly. I say "begin" because the process of becoming one's true self is just that—a process. It is not something which happens once and is done for all time. A man's commitment to hope is a choice which must be constantly renewed. For we hope for what we do not have as yet, in its fullest and most complete sense.

This criterion is the loneliest of them all. No man can ever use it to judge another man's answer. No man can know what barriers or difficulties another man may face in becoming himself. The requirement is for a man to judge himself.

It is these three guides that I point to when I ask myself why I believe that Jesus Christ is God. Of course, they do not give me certainty. I have no objective proofs. Hope as a way of life is a fundamental belief that life is worth living. And this sort of hope ultimately rests on faith.

Why faith? Isn't faith simply believing what you don't have good reasons to believe? Why introduce faith at this point?

The answer is that I am not introducing anything new at all, but putting a new label on the *commitment* we have been talking about all along. Faith is not simply believing something one doesn't have good grounds to believe. It is a fundamental commitment of one's self which, though it may involve a going beyond "evidence" in the usual sense, is the ground of all the activities of a meaningful life, including our reasoning.

We must ask ourselves, "Does not all meaning depend upon faith? Does not a meaningful life require faith in other people, faith in your wife, faith in everyday experiences, faith in the special experiences which point to hope?" If so, then hope as a way of life requires faith as a way of life. If my life is unified, the extension of faith to God is the logical extension of that principle which I employ in each individual area of experience to my existence as a whole.

My faith in Jesus Christ can best be described as a going beyond (not against) the given evidence on the basis of a personal commitment. It is a commitment of my whole person in response to God's love, and as such it involves my cognitive, emotional and volitional being.

Cognitively expressed, faith is *belief.* In the area of emotional and personal experience, faith is *trust.* Seen in its volitional and social aspects, faith is *love.*

But this is my choice. The God who made man in his own image has given to every man the responsibility of choosing for himself.

Footnotes

chapter 2

[1]Fyodor Dostoevsky, *The Brothers Karamazov* (Baltimore: Penguin Books, 1968), p. 733.

[2]Ibid., p. 743.

[3]Ibid., p. 764.

[4]Albert Camus, *The Stranger* (New York: Vintage Books, 1946), p. 5.

[5]Ibid., p. 45.

[6]Ibid., p. 145.

[7]Albert Camus, *The Plague* (New York: Modern Library, 1948), p. 229.

[8]Ibid., pp. 230-31.

[9]Ibid., p. 117.

[10]Ibid., p. 228.

[11]Ibid., p. 150.

[12]Ibid., p. 229.

[13]Albert Camus, *The Fall* (New York: Vintage Books, 1965), p. 110.

[14]Ibid., p. 133.

[15]Ibid.

chapter 3

[1]Jean Paul Sartre, *Nausea* (New York: New Directions, 1959), p. 57.

[2]Ibid., p. 151.

[3]Albert Camus, *The Myth of Sisyphus and Other Essays* (New York: Vintage Books, 1955), p. 44.

[4]*Nausea*, p. 23.

[5]*The Myth of Sisyphus and Other Essays*, p. 15.

[6]*Nausea*, p. 53.

[7]Ibid., p. 152.

[8]Ibid., p. 158.

[9] Ibid., p. 162.

[10] Ibid., p. 163.

[11] Ibid., p. 205.

[12] Jean Paul Sartre, *Being and Nothingness* (New York: Washington Square Press, 1966), p. 448.

[13] Ibid., p. 728.

[14] *Nausea*, p. 116.

[15] Ibid., p. 173.

[16] Ibid., p. 57.

[17] *The Myth of Sisyphus and Other Essays*, p. 15.

chapter 4

[1] Joseph Heller, *Catch-22* (New York: Dell Publishing Co., 1962), p. 46.

[2] Ibid., p. 47.

[3] Fyodor Dostoevsky, *Notes from Underground* (New York: New American Library, 1961), p. 105.

[4] Ibid., p. 110.

[5] Ibid., p. 111.

[6] Ibid., p. 112.

[7] Ibid., p. 113.

chapter 5

[1] Viktor E. Frankl, *Man's Search for Meaning* (New York: Washington Square Press, 1963), p. 156.

[2] Ibid., p. 210.

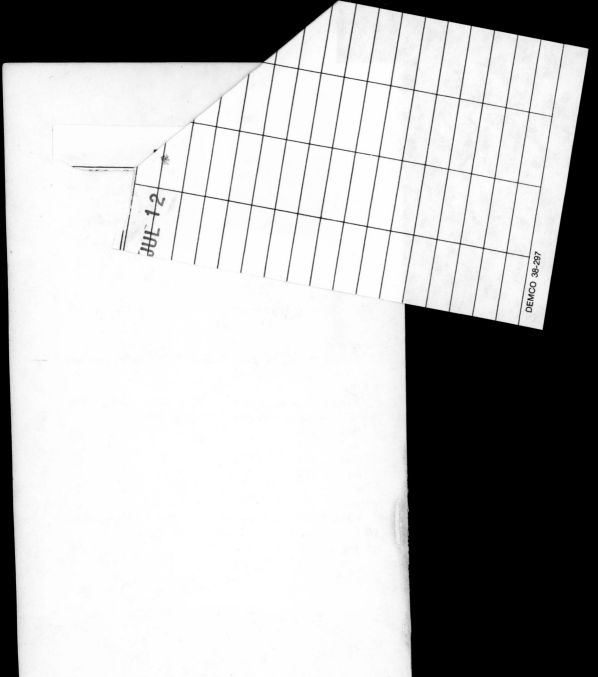

JUL 12

DEMCO 38-297